THE ART OF
POLYMER CLAY
Millefiori Techniques

THE ART OF
POLYMER CLAY
Millefiori Techniques

Projects and Inspiration for
Creative Canework

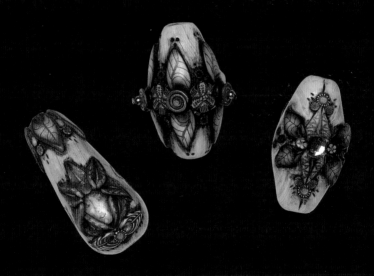

DONNA KATO

PHOTOGRAPHY BY VERNON EZELL

WATSON-GUPTILL PUBLICATIONS

NEW YORK

When working with polymer clay and other suggested products and tools, readers are strongly cautioned to follow the manufacturers' instructions and warnings. If you are pregnant or have any known or suspected allergies, you may want to consult a doctor about possible adverse reactions before using any suggested products or performing any procedures outlined in this book. The techniques and materials described in this book are not intended for children.

Photos: Page 1, pendant by Donna Kato. Page 2 top, bracelet by Judy Belcher; middle, floral earrings by Susan Mueller; bottom, bracelet by Donna Kato. Page 3, beads by Karen Lewis (Klew). Page 6 top, bracelet by Cynthia Tinapple; middle, butterfly by Lynne Ann Schwarzenberg; bottom, fish trophies by Donna Kato. Page 7 top, earrings by Sarah Shriver; middle, decoration jar by Donna Kato; bottom, pin by Wendy Wallin Malinow. Pages 10, 30, 54, 106, and 134, all items by Donna Kato. All of the photographs in this book were taken by Vernon Ezell except: page 5, author photo by Mike Troxler; page 8 top, photo by Robert Diamante; page 9, photo by Paulo Almeida; page 27 top, photo by Melanie West; page 27 bottom, photo by Irit Cohen; page 33, photo by George Yanigihara; page 136, photo by Naama Zamir.

Executive Editor: Joy Aquilino
Editor: Laaren Brown
Production Manager: Alyn Evans
Designer: Areta Buk/Thumb Print

First published in 2008 by Watson-Guptill Publications,
an imprint of the Crown Publishing Group,
a division of Random House, Inc., New York
www.crownpublishing.com
www.watsonguptill.com

Library of Congress Control Number: 2008930442

ISBN-13: 978-0-8230-9918-4
ISBN-10: 0-8230-9918-0

Printed in China

First printing, 2008

1 2 3 4 5 6 7 8 9 / 15 14 13 12 11 10 09 08

For being the only one in the house who goes to the grocery store . . . for understanding that I don't cook, and then cooking . . . for taking care of Doc and Zoe, Ditto and the horses and home . . . for doing laundry and only shrinking a few things . . . for making me laugh . . . for many trips to and from the airport . . . for never, never saying "You can't" . . . for making the impossible possible.

For making me believe in possibilities, shooting books, unflagging support and encouragement, I thank and dedicate this book to my husband, Vernon Ezell, the best life partner anyone could ever have.

Love, D

ACKNOWLEDGMENTS

Thank you Robert Augur, Tony Aquino, Ruben Castaneda, Amaryllis Rodriguez of Van Aken International, and Suzanne Hammond, without whom there would be no Kato Polyclay.

To the wonderful and talented Daniel Torres Mancera and Natalia Garcia de Leaniz, who have shared their home and their hearts. To Carlos Lima, Cristina Almeida and Paulo, and Eugenio Guedes and family, who so kindly extended their friendship in Portugal. To Akira Ikeda, Bruce and Yoshiko Osborne, Miyake-san and the Nisshin Company, seeing Japan was a dream come true, all thanks to you. To Helen Cox and Stephen Smith, dear British friends for so long. To Eti and Moti Raz for opening their home and making their home mine in Israel. To Louise Cozzi and G. for the invitation to teach and stay with them at their lovely home in Stresa.

Thank you to friends Karen Brown, Lani, Alan and Mari Chun, Auntie Xian, Sarah and Guy Chinen, Darlene Clark, Irit Cohen, Peg Monteith, Margaret Harper, Kim Korringa, Irit Levy, Kathy Weaver, Kasey Larson and Jackie of More Than Memories, Leslie at the Bead Garden. To Florida friends Nancy, Sandie, Diana, Mary, Rhonda, Richard, and Gail. To the fabulous foursome Brurya, Iris, Pinky, and Tunia. To Naama Zamir, Paula, and Be. To Ana, Marivi, Ines, and Nati. To Hiroko-chan, Masako-san, Kyoko-chan, and George.

Thanks to Sheila and Bob Miller, Mary and Leo Fassler, Jeanne and Dave Sturdevant, Barb and Gary VerniLau, Emi Fukushima, Debbie and Peter Anderson, Irene Niehorster and Lee Scott, Donna Lopez and Earl

Grey, Connie Sheerin and Ken Williams, Rai Nelson, Carol Hess, Diane Luftig, Jill and Tom Kershner, and others who have taken such good care of me as I've traveled and taught.

To my good friends and compadres in clay and Carnivals Judy Belcher, Leslie Blackford, Kim Cavender, Cathy Johnston, Sue Kelsey, Gail Ritchie, Maria Del Pinto, and Jacqueline Lee, thank you for being the go-to girls who wouldn't know how to let anyone down and always give 100 percent.

Special thanks to the artists/friends who allowed their work to be included in this book.

To Miss Carol Duvall, Kelly Ehrlich, Karen Thomas, and Mary O'Neil. The show may be over, but we're not!

Thank you to Joy Aquilino, Laaren Brown, Areta Buk, and everyone at Watson-Guptill, the best book publishers in the world (just my opinion!)—and undoubtedly the most patient.

To my family, Mom, Alan and Gwen, Tina and Harry, Mark and Kathy, and my nephews Mitchell, Eric, Aaron, Jacob, Sam, and Joshie, and only niece, Hannah.

To my best and oldest friends, Terri Silverstone (and David Lissner) and Mary Prchal.

For my good friends I've lost this year—Eileen Loring and Jacque Ducharme.

And finally, thank you to all my students here and abroad who have taught me so much more than I could ever teach you.

CONTENTS

INTRODUCTION

In 1994, I saw millefiori art for the first time, in Nan Roche's book *The New Clay*. Before that time, I had played with polymer clay many times, making loads of fun things. But when I saw the work of such polymer-clay artists as Kathleen Dustin, Kathleen Amt, Pier Voulkos, Sarah Shriver, and City Zen Cane, a new phase in my work began. Pieces by these artists altered the very way I viewed polymer clay and its potential as an art material. Pictures in clay, can you imagine that?

Looking back, I can see how far we have come with polymer clay. New techniques such as the Skinner Blend, Mike Buesseler's "clay chopping," and other innovations have improved our ability to make amazing millefiori canes and to make our pictures in clay. Today's canes have more shading and more style, and they are much more sophisticated than we ever dreamed of just ten years ago.

Now I am happy to share what I have learned about polymer clay and millefiori techniques over the years in this new book, *The Art of Polymer Clay Millefiori Techniques*. It contains some of my favorite pieces—some made by me, some made by my talented fellow artists—all presented in simple step-by-steps with clear photographs. Start at the beginning and you'll soon see that anyone can make great millefiori canes!

Beginning with a new medium always presents question upon question. It takes time and work to integrate and use all the bits of newly acquired information. When I began work on this book, I wanted to fill in those blanks and also provide my readers with the means to solve problems on their own. I hope that this book will offer a personal polymer clay class for you and for every reader, and that when you have taken each step along the way, you'll share my love of this incredible medium.

Millefiori is one of my favorite techniques. I hope you enjoy this adventure into one of the most exciting techniques in the polymer clay repertoire.

TOP LEFT: KATHLEEN DUSTIN
Rich color effects are hallmarks of Kathleen's work.

LEFT: Z. KRIPKE
Z's petroglyph necklace was made many years ago— the design and her skill as a caner make it as relevant and wearable today.

CRISTINA ALMEIDA
Cristina is a talented artist from Portugal. In this piece she incorporates canes, crystals, texture, wire, and net to make a dramatic statement.

POLYMER CLAY
BASICS

Don't be afraid of polymer clay! I have never met anyone who has enjoyed immediate success with the medium—trial and error are part of the process of discovery. The following pages will give you a basic understanding of polymer clay, from how to choose it to how to use it. Here are explanations of the different brands of clay, descriptions of tools and materials you need to work with polymer clay, information on how to prepare the clay for work, and directions on curing your pieces. Once you understand the basics and try working with the clay using basic techniques, success is sure to follow with piece after beautiful piece. Enjoy your newfound talent!

CHARACTERISTICS OF POLYMER CLAY

KIM CAVENDER
Kim's whimsical clock, designed to raise awareness of breast cancer, features Skinner Blend leaves.

ALL BRANDS OF POLYMER CLAYS are manmade modeling materials composed of the same basic building materials: gels, fillers, plasticizers, coloring agents, and resins. When combined, these ingredients yield polymer clay.

With stiffer European regulations applied to materials deemed "toys" and recent passage of safety legislation in California, several polymer clay companies have recently reformulated their polymer clays. The ingredients that caused the concern—phthlates—have been removed by Van Aken (Kato Polyclay) and Eberhard Faber (Fimo). As of this writing, Polyform has not reformulated its Sculpey/Premo brands.

The new formulations may differ from their phthlate versions in some ways, but they remain polymer clays, working and performing as they always have. You may find one brand softer than it used to be, or the curing temperature might not be the same; but essentially, they are still oven-cured modeling materials—polymer clays.

Unlike earth clays, polymer clays are produced in a great range of colors that may be mixed to create a custom color palette. All brands can be mixed together, although the wisdom of making such mixtures depends on how they will be used. For example, if you are sculpting and wish to strengthen one brand or improve on its blending characteristics, you can freely mix brands with no resulting ill effect. In the case of millefiori caning, it is generally best to use one brand or the same mixture *only* in each cane made. Prior to mixing large amounts of different brands, it is wise to mix a small sample first.

Bringing malleable polymer clay to its permanent hardened state requires exposure to temperatures from 230° to 325° Fahrenheit, depending on the specific brand. Once cured, the clay is "fixed"—that is, it will not return to its original soft state. The period of time when the clay is warm out of the oven is its most fragile state (in most brands), and it is at this time that pieces are most likely to break when handled. Sculpey III, Premo, Fimo, and Fimo Soft should be allowed to cool completely before handling. Kato Polyclay can be handled and even reshaped to some degree when warm with no breakage or cracking. Generally speaking, clay is less likely to break if you wait until after it has cooled to handle it.

All clays must be conditioned. There is some controversy about the importance of conditioning, but I have found that in order to achieve maximum strength and the strongest piece-to-piece adhesion, conditioning is a must. Simply put, conditioning is the act of restoring the clay to a state close to its original factory-mixed condition. Conditioning may be accomplished by kneading and mixing the clay by hand, or by rolling the clay repeatedly, then folding and rolling it through a pasta machine until it is soft and pliable. The pasta-machine method is preferable as kneading may introduce air pockets into the clay.

The easiest clay to condition is Sculpey III, followed by Premo, then Kato Polyclay and Fimo Soft, then Fimo, the most difficult. The ease of conditioning should not be the primary criteria used when selecting a brand of clay, as the easiest to condition may also be the weakest or the most difficult to handle and work with.

Polymer clays are subject to change with prolonged exposure to temperatures of 90°F or higher. But even at cooler temperatures, polymer clay will naturally "advance," or change over time. Advancing makes the clay stiffer, as ingredients shift toward their original wet or dry states. Stored at cool temperatures and away from direct sunlight, polymer clay will last for years.

LEFT: DONNA KATO
I call this my Cha-Cha Bracelet. It's quite simple, just slices cut from a large cane, shaped, drilled, and strung.

ABOVE: EILEEN LORING
This Zuni bear features canes artfully arranged by the late artist Eileen Loring.

Simple tools become so much more interesting with millefiori-covered handles.

The phrase "open time" refers to the time in which the clay remains soft and pliable after conditioning. Certain clay brands "cool down" more rapidly than others and might require reconditioning as you work. It seems there is a relationship between the ease of conditioning and open time, since the easiest clays to condition seem to have the longest open time. Fimo is the exception, because it is the most difficult to condition, but it has a fairly long open time before it needs reconditioning. Reconditioning your canes may be required if they sit for long periods of time. They can be restored by exerting pressure on the sides of the cane, working gently until the cane feels soft all the way through. Depending on the brand, very old canes may become dry and break when cut, making reconditioning a necessity.

Clays differ in terms of strength and flexibility after curing. Although Sculpey III might be the easiest to condition, it is also the most brittle and the weakest of the clays. In my experience, Premo is both weak and strong, as certain colors are very durable while others are brittle and easily broken. Fimo Soft is strong when newly cured but, over time, becomes more brittle. Fimo is a very strong clay that maintains its strength over time. The most durable of these clay brands is Kato Polyclay, which can be repeatedly bent without cracking and does not tear. The stronger the clay, the thinner you may cut slices to be baked as they are.

The degree of flexibility of cured clay differs from brand to brand. The rigidity of cured clay increases with increased clay thickness. I'd suggest trying them all and deciding for yourself which clay best suits your needs. Many polymer clay artists use a range of brands, selecting a particular brand for a specific purpose.

As they are polymers, you'll want to avoid chemical reactions that might occur when the clay is exposed to other polymers. If you drop raw clay on your carpet and leave it there, you might find it melting into your carpet! If you work on fine furniture, you might find raw clay melting into the finish, ruining it. Take proper precautions to protect surfaces.

In the same way, application of certain glazes to a cured item may actually create a chemical reaction between glaze and clay. Should this occur, the glaze won't dry or harden, and your work will eventually dissolve into a sticky mess. This reaction usually takes about a week to reveal itself, so if you're unsure about whether a reaction might occur, be patient and test a piece first before glazing all your work.

In its raw state, polymer clay will adhere to itself, making it unnecessary to use special adhesive agents to join pieces. Firm but gentle pressure will do the job; bonding occurs by curing. The bond between raw to cured clay can be strengthened by brushing a thin layer of liquid polymer clay at the site where the two clays will be joined.

Although polymer clay may be cured many times, you might find that color shifting (or change) may occur, depending on the brand of clay you are using. If the brand is prone to color shift, you may need to use foil to shield parts that have been previously cured.

Certain brands are more prone to this color change from raw to cured state, some shifting as many as three shades, the colors darkening. Brands that shift the least are Kato Polyclay (most Kato Polyclay colors do not change at all) and Fimo and Fimo Soft, which change minimally. If you use a clay brand whose colors are subject to radical change, you'll want to experiment with adding white (usually) to compensate for this characteristic color change.

While polymer clay will adhere to itself, certain polymer clay designs that have minimal clay-to-clay contact may still require the use of a structural armature such as thick wire.

Polymer clay does not bond permanently to anything but itself. For that reason, if your design incorporates metal objects, such as metal clay, bear in mind that these elements must be glued in place after curing with two-part epoxy or some other strong glue.

Because of the low curing temperatures for polymer clay, a great many existing items may be covered with clay, then cured in the oven. Glass, ceramic, papier-mâché, and many plastics may be cured in the oven. Covering pens is a very popular project, but not all pens will survive the curing process. Clear, hard

BELOW LEFT: RICHARD BASSETT
Here is a big bead using Richard's signature caned eyeball.

BELOW: SARAH CHINEN
Sarah is a talented artist from Hawaii. I love her use of color and pattern in these pieces.

plastic such as the inexpensive Bic Round Stic will melt in the oven, while pens such as the Paper Mate FlexGrip handle the curing temperature quite nicely, with no resulting warping or shrinkage. Once again, experimentation is recommended before you invest time and energy creating the perfect polymer clay pen. If you're unsure if a pen may be safely covered, simply remove the ink cartridge and bake the empty pen case for ten minutes at the recommended curing temperature for the polymer clay you are using. If you are covering an object that is not rigid (papier-mâché, for instance) you should use a clay that will withstand flexing without breaking—Sculpey III would not be a good choice as it is brittle and will break if the form beneath flexes.

Glass will, of course, be unaffected by the low curing temperatures used for polymer clay, and you will find that clay sticks easily to its smooth, untextured surface. Bear in mind that clay and glass do not form a permanent bond, so if you, for example, press a cane slice to a wine glass and bake, the piece will not be permanently attached. For a lasting bond, remove the piece after curing and glue it back on with an adhesive such as E-6000 (a silicone-based glue) or two-part epoxy. The best technique is to trap the covered item in clay—for example, completely cover a votive candleholder whose sides curve out from a smaller-diameter bottom, then curve in to a smaller-diameter opening.

Covering a porous or textured piece with clay requires the application of a sealer before covering the object with clay. I've used some heat-set paints for this purpose, or you may use PVA glue or Sobo glue or even a coat of liquid clay (cure it before adding clay elements). Wood can be difficult to cover even when a sealer has been applied. The best wood forms, very fine-grained and free of knots, are

SHARON OHLHORST
For these pieces, Sharon used cane slices to cover real eggs. The shape of an egg makes it necessary to either reduce canes or trim large cane slices as you cover the ends.

from Walnut Hollow. Wood is porous, so when heated, it expands and may create cracks in curing clay on its surface.

The most difficult part of covering most existing forms is doing so without creating air pockets between the item and the clay. When air pockets are heated, the air expands and the offensive air pocket enlarges, causing cracking and damage. To avoid this, carefully inspect anything you cover with clay prior to curing. If you see an air pocket, press the bubble to the nearest opening and expel the air. When I wrap a form with a sheet, I gently stretch the clay as I wrap, and this seems to help quite a bit.

The presence of air pockets in solid clay items such as beads can cause cracks, so it is important to expel air from base clay (the clay that forms the core of the beads before embellishing). Should you find a crack in the cured bead, you may heal the crack by pressing (while the clay is still warm) the sides of the crack together until the bead is cool or by plunging the hot bead into ice water while pressing the crack closed. Artist Leslie Blackford recommends wrapping a cracked piece in a towel and allowing it to cool very gradually.

Cured items will exhibit matte, satin, or even shiny finishes, depending on the brand you are using. Sculpey III is the most matte; Premo, Fimo, and Fimo Soft cure to a satin-type sheen; and Kato Polyclay takes on a shinier appearance. If you wish to matte the finish of Kato Polyclay, simply rub the warm item with a soft towel, or dust the raw item with cornstarch, or even cure the piece buried in cornstarch. For an extremely matte black finish, sand Kato Polyclay with coarse sandpaper (150 or 200 grit), then either return the piece to the oven for five minutes or heat the sanded surface with a heat gun.

Interior armatures should be used when clay walls exceed 1 inch thick or if you are making very large beads or figures. Most commonly used materials are wire and compressed foil, but I know of people who use burned-out lightbulbs and other such items for this purpose, leaving the armatures within the piece. Armatures of this sort will ensure complete curing of clay, will decrease the amount of clay required, will lighten the weight of the finished piece, and in figures and sculptures, can make the piece more structurally sound.

BARBARA SPERLING
Barbara is a master caner and artist. Look at these amazing heron earrings!

MARYLU ELLIOTT
These charming canes show MaryLu's skill and sense of humor.

BRANDS OF POLYMER CLAY

AS YOU'VE DISCOVERED, polymer clay brands differ in a great many ways. Try them all and decide which brand works best for your applications. Do you live in a warm climate or cool, do you have hot hands or cold? These may be factors in your choice of polymer clay. Let's look at some brands and see how they compare to Kato Polyclay.

The newest brand of polymer clay, Kato Polyclay, is the first polymer clay designed by an artist for artists and is the result of a collaboration between Van Aken International and me. We manufacture in Rancho Cucamonga, California.

After discussing the characteristics we wished to have in our clay, Tony Aquino and Van Aken vice president Robert Augur formulated Kato Polyclay. Unlike any of the other brands, Kato Polyclay is vacuum extruded; this process removes most bothersome air pockets in the clay.

Like other brands, Kato Polyclay can be mixed to create new colors. The clay comes in just seventeen colors plus four Color Concentrates: red, yellow, green, and blue. Designed within the line are true complementary colors, which make it possible to mix virtually any color. Kato Polyclay is sold in 2-ounce and 12.5-ounce bars. Kato Polyclay cures from 275 to 325°F. Generally, I cure my pieces at 300°F, reducing curing time by half. All of the pieces and projects in this book are made of Kato Polyclay.

For two years, I consulted on and marketed Fimo and Fimo Soft Clays in the U.S. market, working with Eberhard Faber GmBH, Amaco, and Accent Import. Like Van Aken, these fine companies produce their clay in a very controlled environment to very tight specifications. Their original clay, Fimo, was introduced to the U.S. approximately thirty years ago. Fimo Soft was formulated to address the conditioning comments of polymer clay users. Fimo Soft colors are bright and clear but do shift more than Fimo, as the colors are set in a translucent base. Fimo and Fimo Soft now carry recommended temperatures of 230°F.

KPC and Fimo are just two of a wide variety of polymer clay brands.

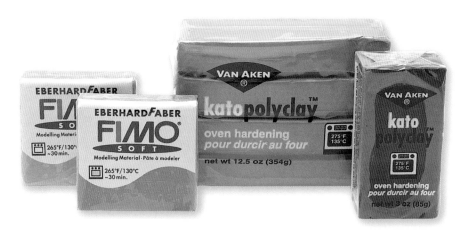

Until 2002, there was only one American manufacturer of polymer clay: Polyform Products Co. The brands they currently produce are Sculpey (also marketed under the Polyform brand name), Super Sculpey, Sculpey III, Premo Sculpey, and several novelty clays. Sculpey III is sold in 2-ounce bars. Premo Sculpey is sold in 2-ounce and 1-pound bars. Sculpey/Polyform is sold in large bulk packages. Polyform clays cure at 275°F.

There are other brands such as Cernit, Modello, Formello, and Creall Therm, but they are more difficult to locate in the U.S. market, and I have no experience with their characteristics.

BRANDS OF LIQUID POLYMER CLAY

Kato Clear Medium is almost crystal clear when it is cured at 325°F. In terms of consistency, it is thinner than Liquid Sculpey, and so it is less prone to troublesome air bubbles. Kato Clear Medium is also easier to sand than Liquid Sculpey. When cured at high heat (between 320 and approximately 340°F), the surface of Kato Clear Medium takes on a high gloss and reaches glasslike clarity.

Introduced by Eberhard Faber, Liquid Fimo is the newest of the liquid polymer clays. Of all the liquid polymers, it begins as the most transparent. Cured Fimo Gel is rubbery, making it the most difficult to sand.

The first of these "polymer clays in a bottle" came from Polyform Products. Liquid Sculpey is thick and milky. After curing, it does clear, but of all brands, it is the least transparent.

All of the liquid polymers work in basically the same way and can be used in the same techniques. All will transfer inkjet images and may be tinted with oil paints, mica pigment powders, and solvent-based inks, such as Tim Holtz's Alcohol Inks (from Ranger Industries) and Piñata inks (manufactured by Jacquard).

With respect to use in caning, liquid clay may be used to soften hard clays, if necessary. For onlay of caned elements, a light application between either a raw or cured base and the cane to be applied will improve the strength of the bond.

REPEL GEL

Repel Gel prevents clay from sticking to other clay. Formulated by Tony Aquino, Repel Gel is an effective resist either wet or dry. Because it is applied as a gel, by finger or by brush, it is easy to target specific areas where clay-to-clay adhesion is unwanted. After the item has been cured, simply wash off the Repel Gel with water.

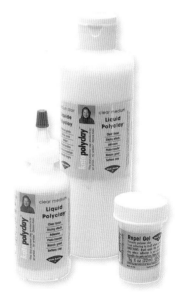

TOP: DONNA KATO
Kato Clear Medium was applied to ensure that the caned elements in this piece, Leslie's Blackbird Goes to Hawaii, *were held securely in place.*

BOTTOM: *Kato Liquid Polyclay and Repel Gel are useful in many applications.*

POLYMER CLAY TOOLS AND MATERIALS

SOME TOOLS I regard as essential, while others are only used incidentally in my work. Very few tools are required for millefiori canes.

Protecting your furniture is of paramount importance, so you'll want to begin with a good work surface. The work surface I use most is a Formica sink hole—that is, the hole cut out of a countertop. Its lightly textured surface allows me to lift even the thinnest sheet without risk of tearing or stretching the sheet.

There are times you might want your clay to stick to the work surface. At these times, you might use a pane of tempered glass or a ceramic tile. Another good all-around option is an acrylic board (lightweight and perfect for travel). When teaching, small ceramic tiles, index cards, or manila folders are easy-to-obtain work surfaces for your students.

HANDLING CLAY

I think my most valuable tool, next to my hands, is my pasta machine. With it, I condition my clay, make Skinner Blends, and roll out uniform sheets of clay. (This type of pasta machine should not be confused with the machines that mix and make pasta!) There are several brands of these hand-crank machines: Makin's, Atlas, Al Dente, Imperia, Pasta Queen. Pasta machines have thickness settings. Atlas and Makin's machines begin with 1 (thickest) and go up to 6 to 9 (thinnest). The other pasta machines sometimes have settings that are just the opposite, with 1 being the thinnest and higher numbers representing thicker settings.

Ceramic tiles, a glass sheet, a marble tile—any of these can make a good work surface. Use a rubber mat underneath to hold the surface in place.

Pasta machines are not made for polymer clay use—they are, of course, made to roll sheets of pasta. Clay is stiffer and firmer than pasta, and so when we roll clay through these machines, we are subjecting the machines to greater stress than they were meant to withstand. For this reason, be kind to your machine and roll sheets of clay through that are already close to the thickness setting, rather than forcing very thick slabs of clay through radically thinner settings.

It is possible to disassemble and clean the machines, but I do not frequently do so. I do, however, take my machine apart at least once to remove the top plates, because they are not essential to machine function. *Do not remove the bottom scraper plates.* After the top plates are out of the way, it is possible to gently remove clay that has collected. To prevent damaging the plates, you should never insert a metal tool (such as a needle tool) to pry out and remove clay from between the rollers and the plates. Instead, use a bamboo skewer for this purpose, gently and carefully easing the clay out. Once the excess clay has been removed, roll light-colored scrap clay through the machine to pick up any remaining bits of clay. The surfaces of the rollers may be cleaned by pressing an alcohol-saturated paper towel or alcohol wipe on them as you crank the machine. Frequent wiping of the lower plates also helps minimize contamination from clay that has been rolled through previously.

On my pasta machine, I've connected a pasta-machine motor. This motor makes it possible for me to use both hands to handle my clay as it is fed into and out of the machine. Recently I added a foot pedal, so now I don't even have to turn the pasta-machine motor on and off by hand—just a press of the pedal and the machine's rollers start turning. There are several brands of motors. I use both the Makin's Clay and Atlas motors.

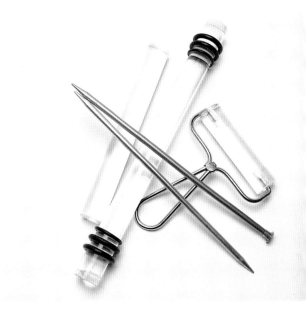

Knitting needles, acrylic rods, the Pro Clay roller (with rubber end rings), a brayer—all of these tools are useful for shaping polymer clay canes.

Acrylic rods are also used to flatten and compress clay for conditioning, to embed cane slices, and to smooth the surfaces of items you are working on. The rods are sold in most craft, art supply, and hobby stores. Thick double-pointed knitting needles are also excellent smoothing tools. When smoothing the surface of a caned piece, use a rolling motion—that is, roll the rod back and forth—rather than a "scraping" motion that might smear the surface of the cane. Handled acrylic brayers are also useful for smoothing surfaces and for instances where you might want to square the sides of a square or rectangular cane, or reduce it.

Cutting and slicing clay can be done with a craft knife, but a better option is a polymer clay blade or, for small canes, a single-edged razor blade. Prior to the introduction of polymer clay blades, the blade most used was a medical tissue-slicing blade. This blade is 4 inches long, sharp, and flexible. The stiffer Kato Nublade, 6 inches long, was introduced to the polymer clay community by Prairie Craft Co. and has gained wide acceptance among polymer clay artists.

Although this blade is more rigid, it is no less sharp. The increased rigidity makes it easier to cut and slice through large blocks or canes with minimal torque and twisting. The Kato Nuflex Blade is also 6 inches long, but it is less

The Kato Marxit measuring tool and special polymer clay cutting blades are useful.

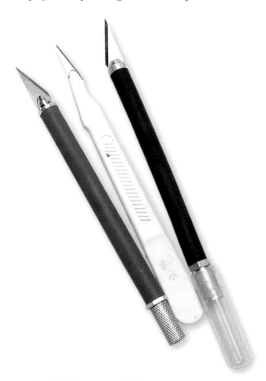

Craft knives or surgical scalpels make it easy to get clean-cut slices from a cane.

rigid, more like the original tissue blade with the addition of 2 inches to its length. The Kato T Blade is comparable to the tissue blade but, like the Nuflex Blade, is made of stainless steel.

Extreme caution should be taken when using any blades of this sort. *These blades are intended for use by adults only and should never be given to children.* When using these blades, the most important rule is to look at the blade before picking it up. Always avoid placing your fingers on any edge of the blade, sharp or dull; rather, grasp the sides of the blade and cut down. In all my years working with these blades, I have never cut myself with them. Be careful, and you will stay safe, too.

The Kato Marxit is a tool I designed and, with my husband, Vernon, brought to market. It is a six-sided ruler, each side measuring different increments in millimeters. The ridges are raised, so when the tool is pressed to the side of a cane or pressed to a sheet of clay, the measurements are transferred into the clay. Among its many uses, the Kato Marxit makes it easy to cut cane slices of uniform thickness.

Rulers minimize waste, particularly in caning. When making canes, you will find many cases in which a cane will be divided, then reassembled. Nine times out of ten, unless you have a very good eye, you may think you have cut them exactly in half, only to discover that one half is longer than the other. This means you have wasted some of the original cane.

I usually make bead holes before I bake, so I have many needle tools, of various bore sizes. The Kemper Pro Tool is an excellent basic needle tool. It is inexpensive and available at most craft and hobby stores. The needle is set in a thin metal handle and protrudes out of the handle perfectly straight—very important for "drilling" bead holes. I also use bamboo skewers. You may also make your own needle tools by inserting the eye of a carpet or doll needle into a mass of raw clay, then baking.

There are instances when you will want to drill holes into your pieces after curing. This task will be made simpler by first drilling a fine pilot hole before the piece is cured. This pilot hole will guide the bit through the cured clay.

Curing first, before drilling, eliminates distorted shape or damage to the piece. For drilling into cured clay, I use a hand drill (pin vise) and even drill bits.

Many bead makers drill their bead holes following curing, especially if they are making a large quantity of beads. The electric Dremel tool is commonly used, mounted to its own drill press. Before curing, it is helpful to pierce the raw bead at the place you will want to drill the hole or make a pilot hole in the raw clay.

To achieve a high sheen on finished pieces, you'll need several grits of wet/dry sandpaper. To matte your finished pieces, you'll want coarse-grit sandpapers or sanding blocks and dishwashing scrubbies (coarse green and the finer white) to sand cured clay pieces.

Cyanoacrylate (CA) glue bonds almost instantly with polymer clay and is what I use to secure Buna cord to my jewelry. It is also used to glue pin backs to pieces. There are many brands of CA glues. My preferred brands are my own, Kato Polyglues. One is black and flexible, while the other is odorless and does not fog the surface of the clay. Other suitable glues include two-part epoxies and silicone types such as PVA and GOOP. The polymer clay artist Jacqueline Lee favors Hypo Cement for most of her after-curing glue needs. PVA glues are used to prepare porous surfaces before covering with clay.

Choose the right glue for the application.

Designed by Sue and Gale Lee, Poly-Tools Bead Rollers form perfectly shaped and uniform clay beads. Round, oval, bicones, and other shapes may be made when the Poly-Tools systems are used. Rods of clay may be pressed into the polycarbonate bead rollers to create perfectly rounded tiles for bracelets. Sue and her husband, Gale, have also designed an ingenious bead-baking system, the Pro Bead Rack. Raw clay beads are threaded onto pins. The pins are then placed in notches in the aluminum baking rack.

The Makin's Ultimate Clay Extruder comes with fitted disks that let crafters extrude clay in a wide range of shapes and sizes.

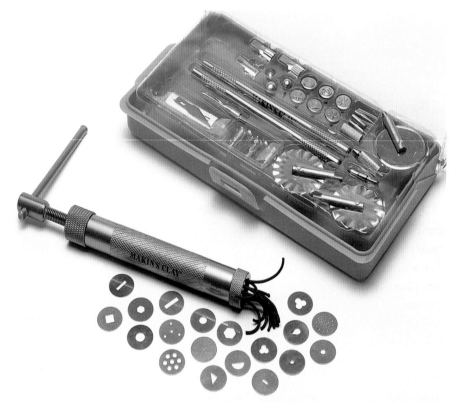

Shape cutters can be useful for cutting cane slices.

A clay gun is needed for the Klimt cane and for other millefiori canes. My favorite is the Makin's Clay clay extruder. This gun self-cleans with a rubber gasket attached to the screw-in plunger. The screw makes extruding even stiff clay a simple task. To use, select a disk (made from stainless steel) and screw it into place. Soften and roll a cylinder of clay and drop it in the barrel. Screw the plunger back onto the barrel and turn the screw to extrude the clay.

I find shape cutters can be a real timesaver; they make simple work of many tasks. Kemper manufactures a comprehensive line of small metal cutters (star, square, round, leaf, posy, and heart) in many sizes, and all with built-in plungers to expel clay. Open-backed metal cookie cutters are an inexpensive option and widely available. Plastic cutters such as those manufactured by Wilton work well with polymer clay. But be careful! I have some plastic cutters from Japan that I must clean after each use. If I don't, a chemical reaction occurs and my cutters start to melt!

I most frequently use my set of graduated circle and oval cutters, and a set of cutters in various simple geometric shapes that are particularly tall. The value of the circle and oval cutters is obvious, while the tall cutters are used for constructing small boxes. If you want to round the corners of the clay, use artist Cathy Johnston's tip: Place a sheet of plastic wrap on the clay sheet. Cut through the plastic and the clay. Remove the plastic, and voila—the shape will be rounded at the edges.

For slicing, Valerie Waters and Kathy Shield (ValKat Designs) have introduced their Precise-a-Slice cane slicer. This compact acrylic tool has a backing block that holds one end of a cane steady. The sliding increment bar can be locked and unlocked. One end of the tool features a 90-degree cutting face, while the other features a 45-degree angled cutting face.

Create metallic effects with, from left to right, lose composition leaf, sheet composition leaf, and metal foils in oil slick and rainbow colors.

DONNA KATO
I made this inro by draping clay over a small rock.

Metal leaf may be used in millefiori canes. It works particularly well when set in translucent clay. The least expensive metal leaf, and the easiest to find, is composition leaf. Composition leaf, also called imitation leaf, mimics gold, silver, and copper, and it is available in a variety of patterns. Although metal leaf, like metal, cannot be permanently bonded to polymer clay, metal leaf rarely requires protection when it is used in canes.

Genuine metal leaf is also available. When I am using metal leaf, I prefer 23-karat gold and genuine silver leaf in my work, rather than composition leaf. Genuine metal leaf is softer and less brittle.

Foils offer polymer enthusiasts the possibility of creating brightly colored patterned metal effects. These are frequently used to imitate dichroic (two-color) glass. The foil is made by coating clear mylar—if you see the pattern, you're actually looking through the mylar itself.

The process for securing the foil coating to clay is a simple one. Place the foil on raw clay, pattern side up. If you're looking at a dull silver sheet, it's upside down; you must see the pattern. Using the side of a credit card, quickly stroke the foil—it's sort of a whipping movement. Grasp a corner of the foil and quickly rip it off the clay. The mylar should be clear and the pattern should be left behind on the clay. Not all foils will work. The holographic designs, for example, will not leave the mylar unless they are heated.

For use as draping forms or temporary armatures, I have a growing collection of rocks and ceramic, glass, and metal items. Clay is draped or wrapped over these, and when the clay is cured, the forms are removed. The important characteristic that all of these items share is their resistance to change at clay-curing temperatures.

STORING YOUR CLAY

Polymer clay begins curing at approximately 90°F, so choose the location for storing your clay carefully. Make sure that the clay is kept in a cool place where it will not be exposed to heat or light.

Raw, unwrapped clay may be wrapped with plastic wrap or placed in Ziploc-type bags that will keep the clay clean. Some people prefer to wrap their canes in wax paper; I don't, as I have had canes dry up this way.

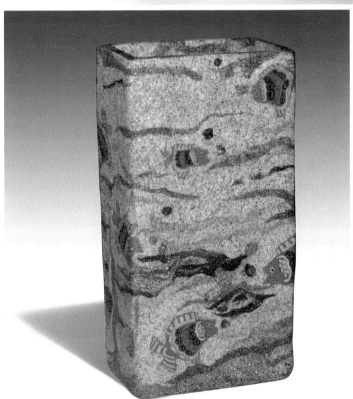

ABOVE: MELANIE WEST
These beautiful bowls were created by pressing thick-cut cane slices on an existing form.

LEFT: IRIT COHEN
Israeli artist Irit Cohen adds bright caned fish to her clay-covered vessel.

Certain plastics, generally the hard, clear kinds, react with raw clay. If such a chemical reaction occurs, the clay "melts" into the plastic, making a sticky mess. I store my canes in plastic boxes that bear the recycle number 5. This number appears on the bottom of most of these translucent, flexible boxes, such as the ones that are used to hold fishing tackle. The late artist Eileen Loring, from Colorado, discovered ammo shell storage cases, and these are ideal for storing small canes.

CURING YOUR CLAY AND SAFETY

Curing polymer clay requires exposure to temperatures ranging from 230° to 325°F. Each brand has its own recommended curing time and temperature,

Boxes used for storing fishing tackle, Matchbox cars, and ammunition are just the right size for holding canes.

and the manufacturer's recommendations should be followed to the letter. In order to achieve the maximum strength, the recommended temperature must be reached. For this reason, it is best to make your canes out of one brand of clay.

Invest in an oven thermometer and a timer. With the thermometer, you can determine the accuracy of your oven temperature gauge. You should know this before you cure anything! When I cure my pieces, I leave the thermometer in the oven, checking it occasionally.

With many ovens, you do not need a separate timer—the oven has its own, and you can set the timer to turn on with the oven and turn off when the time runs out. If your oven does not have this helpful feature, get a timer to ensure that your pieces are not cured too long. In some brands, extended curing will have little to no effect on your work; others can be damaged by the heat. Kato Polyclay is largely unaffected by extended curing time, while Polyform clays will darken and change.

I have a convection oven that I use only for curing polymer clay. I believe that occasional use of a regular home oven—the one you use for cooking food—poses no threat to your family's health, but there are those who would disagree! Toaster ovens are a last resort. The cooking chamber of the average toaster oven is small and narrow, placing the clay in close proximity to the heating elements. Toaster ovens are also prone to temperature spiking.

I have used an electric frying pan to cure flat pieces with fair results. Specific temperatures may be set when using electric fry pans. If you use a frying pan, place items on a Teflon sheet when baking. The Melt Art Melting Pot, made for Suze Weinberg by Ranger Industries, is perfect for travel and partially curing small pieces. Such pieces should be completely cured later.

If you must use your home oven, I'd recommend constructing a special curing chamber to be placed within the oven itself. To make one, place polyester batting or baking soda inside a baking pan, then place items to be cured in the pan. Nesting the pieces in this way prevents flat, shiny spots on your finished work. Slide the entire pan into a turkey roasting bag. Essentially, you will have created a sealed chamber within the oven, and any residue from polymer outgassing will collect inside the cooking bag, not on the sides of your oven. You may find it necessary to lengthen the curing time.

In addition to baking on polyester batting, I have begun baking beads and other rounded pieces in a nest of cornstarch or baking soda. Place a thick layer of powder in a baking pan and press the pieces into the powder. This "sagger box" offers support to bulky or heavy pieces and minimizes cracking in large items. After curing, remove the piece and, in a bowl of water, brush off the cornstarch with a toothbrush. Let the water evaporate naturally, leaving behind the cornstarch that you may use again. Baking powder isn't as messy as cornstarch, and you can brush the powder off easily without soaking.

Generally it is best to segregate your polymer clay tools from any tools that might be used in food preparation. Although polymer clay is certified AP Non Toxic and has passed rigorous testing in order to earn the ASTM D 4236 certification, it is not meant to be used to make food-bearing items. This means no mugs, no plates, no cups, no bowls—at least not those that you'd eat out of. Decorative items only, please.

When it is used properly, following the manufacturers' curing recommendations, polymer clay is perfectly safe. The only time it might possibly pose a hazard is when it is burned. Most everyone I know has, at one time or another, burned a batch of polymer clay. If this should happen, take the burned-clay items outside, open the windows, and let the air clear before returning. Get your pets outside, too. Certain animals are particularly sensitive to fumes, especially birds. If you have birds, you'll want to make sure they are not near your oven at any time.

Most brands cannot withstand prolonged exposure to temperatures of more than 300°F, with the exception of Kato Polyclay, which cures from 275 to 325°F. If Kato Polyclay is cured at 325°F, the cooking time should be reduced by half. Kato Polyclay cured at this temperature is even stronger than clay cured at 275°F. Certain colors, such as translucent, will darken at these higher temperatures. The curing times given in this book are based on a curing temperature of 300°F, unless otherwise specified.

CLEANUP

I keep a spray bottle of isopropyl alcohol for cleaning my work surface, tiles, and tools. Simply spray and wipe.

After working with polymer clay and definitely before eating, hands should be cleaned thoroughly. Wipe hands with alcohol wipes or lotion, then finish with warm soap and water. It is also helpful to coat your hands with the product called Gloves in a Bottle before working with clay. This "lotion" seals in moisture, while it creates a light barrier on your skin. It makes it much easier to remove clay, paint, or any other messy material from your hands.

INTRODUCTION TO MILLEFIORI

Millefiori is one of the most popular polymer clay techniques. Translated from Italian, the word *millefiori* literally means "thousand flowers" because the cross-cut slices, grouped together, look like a field of beautiful flowers in bloom.

In Italy, millefiori has been associated with art glass for many years. But when polymer clay was first introduced, polymer clay artists such as Pier Voulkos, Kathleen Dustin, and Kathy Amt quickly learned that the millefiori technique could be applied to polymer clay. To make polymer clay millefiori, complex canes—logs or loaves of clay—are created by pressing rods and sheets of colors together to create images or patterns. Then the logs are sliced to reveal the intricate pictures within.

MAKING MILLEFIORI

IN SOME WAYS, polymer clay is even better suited for millefiori than glass is. Without the heat required in glass work, artists can create images of even greater complexity than could be produced in glass. And as with glass, polymer canes can be reduced without losing the original image.

If you are new to this technique, begin by making small, simple canes. Many of us begin with attempts to make elaborate face canes—and for most of us, this is ill advised. Begin with the basics. In no time, you'll be constructing the most complex canes. When you start, it is helpful to make a drawing of the cane you'd like to build, comparing clay elements to the drawing as you construct the cane. This is also the best way to control the size of the canes you make. I generally do not make extremely large canes, preferring to make canes as I need them and thus minimizing storage problems.

Clay selection is important. You would not construct a cane of clays of drastically different softness. A cane constructed of Fimo (hardest) and Sculpey III (softest) would not reduce well, because the Fimo would be more resistant to pressure (and movement) than the Sculpey III, which would move more quickly. A reduced cane made of these two clays would be primarily composed of Fimo with very little Sculpey III remaining, as the Sculpey III would have moved out to the unusable ends during the reduction process.

Although Sculpey III might be initially easier to use and condition, you might find it least suitable to the millefiori technique. The softness can result in a less crisp and less accurate reduction of the original image. For this reason, I'd recommend Kato Polyclay, Fimo, and Fimo Soft when making canes. Premo Sculpey may also be used for cane making, and it works better than Sculpey III, but it tends to heat too quickly. It can also become overly sticky with handling and, unless it is leached between pieces of paper toweling (to remove excess plasticizer) before using, it can become difficult to handle. Again, the end image might be more distorted after reducing.

DONNA KATO
Simple canes were used to create thick, large half-round beads. Once strung, they became this bracelet.

Slicing canes also plays a part in clay selection. If the clay is too soft or too sticky, you may have difficulty cutting clean, thin slices that maintain the shape and patterns of the cane itself. Soft, sticky canes tend to squash down or smear, making it difficult to maintain the original crispness and clarity of the image. Sculpey III and Premo Sculpey tend to squash and smear more than Kato Polyclay, Fimo, and Fimo Soft and usually need to rest for a period of time before cutting, whereas the others may usually be sliced almost as soon as they are made. Still, there are artists who make beautiful canes using Premo and Sculpey III, so it certainly isn't impossible to do so.

Covering a surface with millefiori slices presents its own challenges. When stiffer cane slices are applied to a soft core, the soft clay will fill the spaces between the cane slices; when soft cane slices are applied to a stiffer core, they will move out over the surface and join to fill the air spaces between slices. (With the softer cane, to minimize distortion of the cane image and shape, you'll want to fill the spaces with additional clay.) The best end result comes from using a clay of moderate stiffness, resistant to increasing softness from handling, for both canes and background.

Cane slices may be applied to a prebaked core or to existing forms (glass votives, for example). Unless you first cover the cured base bead with raw clay first, only the cane slices will move, making it more important than ever to fill air spaces between the slices. If you are covering a glass form, try covering the entire form with a layer of clay first, then applying slices. Or make a decorated sheet, then cover the form. Glass, metal, and glazed ceramic forms do not form a permanent bond with polymer clay, so capturing the form in clay will ensure that the clay does not release from the glass after curing. Individual freestanding slices may be baked on the forms, but they will have to be removed and glued back on after curing.

I prefer to use cane slices selectively to create the overall image, only covering entire sheets with canes when I want an overall background pattern. When working in this way, I take a thin slice (always cut slices as thin as possible), position it on the bead or background clay, and smooth it into the surface, one or two slices at a time, never overlapping slices before smoothing. To smooth, I use a large double-pointed knitting needle and, beginning at the edge of the cane, roll it to the clay. I then roll across the rest of the cane to smooth it onto the clay.

When making sheets of overall, repeating pattern, first roll a sheet of base clay. This sheet may be fairly thin—about number 3 or 4 on a Makin's Clay or an Atlas machine. Onto this sheet place thin, uniform slices, fitting and butting them edge to edge to match the pattern.

Once the slices have been positioned on the sheet, slice away the extra clay from thicker slices that rise above the rest of the sheet. Then roll over the joins between slices and sheet with a knitting needle or rod, working both horizontally and vertically, finishing by rolling across the entire sheet with an acrylic rod.

TIP

When making beads, it is best to have a stiffer base clay. This will help maintain the overall shape of the bead you are making. Clay that is too soft gives too easily to applied pressure and in the end will result in distorted cane images or bead shape.

MASAKO INABE

Masako used the component caning technique to create this— my favorite bead.

Work on a ceramic tile or another surface that the clay will "grab" so that the base sheet will not move or enlarge as you roll. The sheet will stick to the tile, but it can easily be removed by forcing a blade under the sheet and sliding it along the tile.

When slices are very thin, be careful when choosing the color of the base sheet. If the slices are extremely thin, the base color may show through the slices. This is especially true of translucent canes, so for those, select white, pearl, or light-colored base clay. Once again, there are no absolutes; you may wish to apply your translucent canes to a colored background for a particular effect. The use of translucent clay with opaque canes can result in beautiful effects, as seen in the work of Kathleen Dustin and Ann Dillon, and in the floral compositions of Leigh Ross.

Complex canes are canes made from many elements to create a whole. I prefer to make component canes instead. Complex canes have the whole pattern within just one cane. Component canes are individual, simple canes (the components), used together to create a complete image on clay.

I tend to make components that may be used in a variety of ways for different effects. My floral pieces actually use one basic technique to make a single petal and a single leaf. Then I use slices cut from these individual component canes to create a finished picture. Component canes need not be complicated. Masks I've made use the most basic canes, but when they are assembled, they offer an object of visual complexity.

When making complex canes that require division and reassembly of parts, remember to cut the waste off the ends of the canes before measuring and dividing (cutting). This will ensure that the finished cane will be good all the way through from one end to the other.

When making canes, pay attention to color and contrast, for although an image might be very clear and distinct in its original form, you might find it almost disappears after reduction. Maximum contrast is found between white and black. A cane composed of the two would hold detail through the smallest reduction.

ABOVE: ANN DILLON
Striking earrings showcase Ann's use of subtle color effects.

RIGHT: LEIGH ROSS
Millefiori canes may be used to make beads for unusual jewelry.

Artist Carol Simmons creates complete pictures by using the simplest of canes rather than creating a whole image in one single cane. She is, in my opinion, one of the most skilled polymer clay artists in terms of her use of color, contrast, and pattern, and in the meticulous construction and finish of her pieces.

The thinnest outline of a contrasting color will help maintain crispness and detail. A thin white wrap will help maintain brightness, while black wrapped around the same color could make the colors appear dull. With translucent clay, this effect is very obvious—black muddies the color, while white brightens the color. So, generally speaking, white wraps translucent. White may also be used as a buffer between black and translucent, and the thinnest sheet of white will do the trick. In some projects, such as face canes, you might wish to have the dark against the face tone, to give the effect of shading. Experimentation is the key here. The more canes you make, the faster you'll discover what works and doesn't work for you.

PACKING

"Packing" is the term for filling areas in and around canes. Spaces are filled by fitting in rods, wedges, and sheets of clay. The more tightly the spaces are packed, the more accurate your reduction will be. It is helpful to wrap specific elements of your design with background color to minimize distortion.

For example, in the case of a face cane, by wrapping the eyes with a sheet of the face color before packing the rest of the face color, you ensure that the lines around the eyes will remain straight and smooth and will not "spike" as the clay packed around fills in. In the case of complete flower canes, for instance, packing the area around the flower with translucent clay can increase the usefulness of a cane, because it does not tie you to a specific color background. If a cane packed with translucent is sliced thinly enough, the translucent will not be apparent against the background color. You may even slice the cane and cut and remove clay around the image.

REDUCTION

Reduction is making the diameter of a cane smaller and smaller. To do this, you want to transfer the pressure you exert around the perimeter to the center of the cane. In order to simplify reduction of large canes, it is helpful to construct canes with a decent height-to-width ratio. If I make a cane 6 inches in diameter, I need to make it a minimum of 3 inches tall. Clay used to make canes of large diameters should not be too heat-responsive. This sort of clay just becomes softer, the clay at the perimeter moving out more and the pressure exerted less likely to affect the center of the cane.

When reducing, do not reduce the entire cane to its smallest size. Work in stages, reserving the cane in different sizes. Canes may always be reduced, but you can't make them large again without creating image distortion. Practically speaking, it is much easier to store unused canes of larger sizes than miles of reduced cane.

CAROL SIMMONS
Carol makes the most beautiful, intricate canes.

COLOR

ABOVE: LINDLY HAUNANI
These beads began as a Skinner Blend bullseye cane with stripes around the center bullseye. Lindly cut and reshaped segments to create this dramatic choker.

RIGHT: JANA ROBERTS BENZON
Jana's mastery of kaleidoscope caning and her use of color are evident in this exotic bracelet.

ONE OF THE MOST APPEALING characteristics of polymer clay is the great variety of colors available. Each brand features different colors, and you may also custom-mix your own colors. In this simple way, you can create you own look, using color to add your own distinctive touch.

An understanding of color and contrast will make all the difference in the success of your canes, so it is well worth your while to engage in some experimentation if you are just beginning.

This section was written by artist Laurie MacIsaac. My color choices tend to be more intuitive, less academic; and so, for your benefit, Laurie graciously wrote this section for me and provided the clay samples to illustrate the concepts.

Her exercises and charts are based on Kato Polyclay. The line was designed for maximum efficiency, featuring seventeen colors from which virtually any color may be made. The eight spectral colors form the foundation for color mixing. We've recently added color concentrates to the line, a product specially designed for color mixing. If these colors were placed on a color wheel, you would find them evenly spaced around. Thank you, Laurie!

COLOR: AN ARTIST'S MOST VALUABLE TOOL

One of the key elements in design is color. Artists have been using color theory for centuries to ensure that their color choices bring out the best in their work. Some artists have a built-in color sense; others have developed it over time. Still others use a color wheel as a tool in order to make the best possible color choices. The colors of Kato Polyclay are based on the traditional color wheel, which allows artists to easily create color palettes and schemes that reflect their personal style. Remember, the instructions in this section refer to Kato Polyclay, the only polymer clay designed for easy and effective color mixing.

THE COLOR WHEEL

Using a color wheel, we can begin to understand the relationships between colors.

A standard color wheel has twelve colors, all derived from the three primary colors: red, yellow, and blue.

The three primary colors, when mixed, create three secondary colors: orange, green, and violet.

The primary and secondary colors, when mixed together, create six tertiary colors: blue-green, blue-violet, red-violet, red-orange, yellow-orange, and yellow-green.

To create the six tertiary colors, you would condition the following colors of Kato Polyclay: red, ultra blue, yellow, orange, violet, green, and magenta. Roll each color to an even thickness. Using a cutter, cut the number of "parts" indicated in the recipe below and fully blend the clay until no streaks remain.

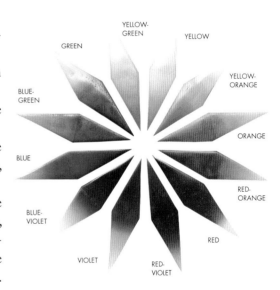

Kato Polyclay color wheel.

blue-green	1 part ultra blue plus 1 part green
blue-violet	1 part ultra blue plus 4 parts violet
red-violet	1 part magenta plus 1 part violet
red-orange	2 parts red plus 5 parts orange
yellow-orange	8 parts yellow plus 1 part orange
yellow-green	24 parts yellow plus 1 part green

Set aside the rest of the magenta clay for another project. You will be left with the twelve standard colors on the color wheel. These colors, mixed with one another and with neutrals such as brown, black, white, and gray, can be used to create any color imaginable.

Understanding the relationships between colors will help you determine which colors work well together.

COLOR CHIPS

When experimenting with clay colors, it's a good idea to keep a record of any color recipe that you like. Making color chips is a fun way to create a valuable tool that will help you choose color schemes for your projects.

To make color chips, roll each of the twelve colors you have just made to an even thickness. (The number 3 setting on a pasta machine works well.) Using a 1-inch circle cutter, cut a color chip out of each of the twelve colors. Using a ¼-inch circle cutter or a straw, punch a hole in the chip for stringing. Bake. Once the chip is cool, write the recipe on the back with a permanent marker, and string the chips onto a piece of Buna cord.

Color chips let artists keep a visual record of their color recipes.

VARIATIONS

Of course there are countless different colors in the world. Here are some simple variations on our color wheel.

For pearl: 1 part color plus 1 or more parts pearl
For pastel: 1 part color plus 1 or more parts white
For muted pastels: 1 part color plus 1 or more parts beige
For translucent: 1 part color plus 1 or more parts translucent
For metallics: 1 part color plus 1 part gold or 1 part silver or ¼ part copper
For deeper colors: 1 part color plus ¹⁄₁₆ part black

MIXING COLOR

USING THE COLOR WHEEL, we can easily see the various color families, or hues, that are available to us—but somehow we never seem to be able to find exactly the color we need. Here are some tricks for adjusting your colors to get the perfect color and shade for your project.

NEUTRALIZING WITH COMPLEMENTS

Let's experiment! Condition and roll to a number 1 thickness on your pasta machine some red and some green Kato Polyclay. Using a 1-inch round cutter, cut several circles from each color. Mix one circle—that is, one part—of each color together. Congratulations, you have created mud! This effect happens whenever colors that are opposite each other on the color wheel, otherwise known as complementary colors, are mixed.

While we don't generally have a need for a lot of mud-colored clay in our work, we can use this predictable result to our advantage. If you ever have a need to tone down or neutralize a color, simply add small amounts of its complement to the clay mix until you achieve the hue or color that you are looking for. Try adding small amounts of red to green (or vice versa) and watch how the color changes.

Colors take different amounts of their complements to neutralize. Since violet is a very saturated color, very little violet is needed to neutralize yellow clay. But a great deal of yellow will be required to neutralize violet clay.

A wonderful palette of neutralized or "dulled" colors can be created by mixing complements together.

The opposite of	So to create the toned-down palette, use
yellow is violet	2 parts yellow plus ¹⁄₁₆ part violet
yellow-orange is blue-violet	2 parts yellow-orange plus ¹⁄₁₆ part blue-violet
orange is blue	2 parts orange plus ¹⁄₁₆ part blue
red-orange is blue-green	2 parts red-orange plus ¹⁄₁₆ part blue-green
red is green	2 parts red plus ¹⁄₈ part green
yellow-green is red-violet	2 parts yellow-green plus ¹⁄₈ part red-violet

Look at this Skinner Blend (see page 107 for more on Skinner Blends) made with red and green clay. Note how intense the colors are at each end and how they gradually neutralize to brown in the middle.

Red clay mixed with other colors to create various tints, tones, and shades. Clockwise from the bottom: red; red mixed with black; red mixed with brown; red mixed with gray; red mixed with white.

ADJUSTING COLORS WITH BLACK, WHITE, BROWN, AND GRAY

Adding black or white to a color adjusts the value of the color. You'll need to add a lot of white to a color to increase its value (that is, to lighten it), or just a little black to decrease its value (that is, to darken it).

Sometimes a color does not need to be lightened or darkened but needs to be a little more earthy. Create rustic tones by adding small amounts of brown to your mix. Dusty colors are achieved by adding white and a small amount of black to the mix.

CREATING THE PERFECT COLOR MATCH

We can take all these tricks and use them to capture a specific color in clay. For this exercise, roll out your clay to an even thickness. Use a cutter to cut parts from each color. Select a target color, perhaps from a paint chip. Then follow these steps to match the target.

1 Take a close look at the target color. Using the color wheel, determine which of the twelve color "families" it belongs to.

2 Which side of the family does the target color favor? Is the red-violet you are trying to create more violet than red? Then add violet, a little at a time, to the clay until you achieve the color that you are looking for.

3 Is the target color duller than my clay? If it is, add small amounts of the clay's complementary color to the mix to dull it.

4 Is the target color lighter or darker than my clay? If the target color is lighter, add small amounts of white. If it is darker, add small amounts of black. Add white or black in very small amounts until you achieve the desired color.

Look closely at the results; you should be fairly close to the target. If not, examine the clay to see what it needs. The most common problem at this point is that you may have added so many other colors to the clay that the main color looks diluted. Try adding more of the main color to the mix.

Once you have achieved the desired color, note the number of parts you used from each clay color. This "recipe" will help you create more of your target color when you are ready to begin your project.

RE-CREATING EARTH TONES

Even browns and grays can lean toward a specific color family. If you are trying to match a brown, examine it closely. It's likely to lean toward yellow, orange, or red. Add two parts of the underlying color to brown. Mix and adjust accordingly with more brown, black, or white, or the underlying color, or its complement.

DESIGNING WITH COLOR

Color schemes are tried-and-true combinations of colors, based on research and experimentation. Don't think of these schemes as "color rules"; instead, use them as starting points for your color design, especially when you've hit a creative block.

MONOCHROMATIC

A monochromatic color scheme uses just one color, any color on the color wheel. The combination of different shades of the color will create excitement and interest. The bigger the difference in shades, the more dramatic the effect. Here, various amounts of black and white were mixed with an ultra blue and pearl mix to create different shades of blue.

MONOCHROMATIC

COMPLEMENTARY

A complementary color scheme uses any two colors that are opposites on the color wheel. Projects using this scheme may have one dominant color, with the other color providing an accent. For this tile, shades of red-violet and yellow-green were used equally.

 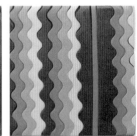

COMPLEMENTARY

SPLIT COMPLEMENTARY

A split complementary color scheme uses three colors. Choose a dominant color for your project; blue was chosen for this tile. The complementary color for blue is orange. This scheme does not use the complementary color, but the colors on either side of it, in this case red-orange and yellow-orange.

SPLIT COMPLEMENTARY

DOUBLE SPLIT COMPLEMENTARY

A double split complementary color scheme uses four colors. Choose two complementary colors such as yellow-green and red-violet. Ignore these colors, but select the colors on either side of both of them—yellow, green, red, and violet.

DOUBLE SPLIT COMPLEMENTARY

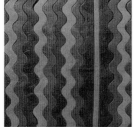

ANALOGOUS

ANALOGOUS

An analogous color scheme uses three colors that lie next to one another on the color wheel—for example, yellow-orange, orange, and orange-red. Analogous colors make wonderful Skinner Blends (see page 107 to learn about Skinner Blends).

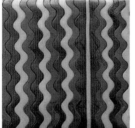

ANALOGOUS/DIRECT COMPLEMENT

ANALOGOUS/DIRECT COMPLEMENT

This color scheme includes the complement of the middle color in the analogous color scheme. Yellow-orange, yellow, and yellow-green were the three analogous colors chosen here. We then added violet, the complement of yellow, to add interest to the tile.

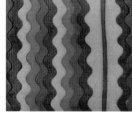

TRIADIC

TRIADIC

The triadic color scheme uses any three colors that are equidistant from one another on the color wheel. The colors used for this tile are red-violet, blue-green, and orange-yellow.

QUADRATIC

The quadratic color scheme uses any four colors that are equidistant from one another on the color wheel. This tile contains yellow-orange, red, blue-violet, and green.

QUADRATIC

CONTRAST

VALUE REFERS TO the lightness or darkness of a color. Adjusting the value of the colors within your project will increase or decrease the contrast in your project. You can use contrast to advance or recede different elements—that is, to bring them forward or push them back visually. Here's the rule of thumb for using contrast: High contrast advances and low contrast recedes.

Following this rule will almost always yield good results when building a cane. For example, if you are making a cane with leaves and a flower and you want the leaves to fade into the background, use low-contrast colors for both the background and the leaves—perhaps dark green leaves in a dark blue background, or light green leaves in a light blue background. If you want the leaves to stand out, use high-contrast colors such as dark green for the leaves and light blue for the background.

If you choose colors that are similar in value for your flower color and background, you can still make an effective cane by wrapping the petals of the flower in a contrasting color before assembling. This is why the instructions for some canes have you wrap each element of the cane with black before assembling. It provides the contrast needed to define the boundaries of the flower.

The two flowers shown below right were built in exactly the same way, except that in the one shown far right, each petal was wrapped in black before assembling. After reduction, you can see that the unwrapped cane looks more like three concentric circles than like a flower with clearly defined petals. Use a different shade of the same color for a softer contrast, as was done for the leaf cane at left.

Knowing how to manage color in your work will give you the control you need to have your project turn out exactly as you had envisioned. Experiment with color to create your own distinctive clay palette that will make your art personal and unique.

 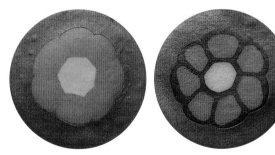

A contrasting background makes the leaves pop; a background color similar to the leaf color gives a softer effect, left.

Wrapping the petals of a flower in black before assembling gives the flower greater definition, right.

MILLEFIORI TECHNIQUES

YOU'RE ALMOST READY TO BEGIN! Working with polymer clay is easy, but there are just a few essential techniques you will need to learn before you begin—conditioning the clay, rolling sheets of clay, storing clay, and curing finished pieces.

CONDITIONING

Before you begin working on canes, you will need to condition your polymer clay. Conditioning brings the clay to its soft, workable, straight-from-the-factory condition. Softer brands such as Sculpey III and Premo may be cut in thick slices from the bar and taken through the pasta machine immediately. Repeated folding and rolling of the sheet will condition the clay. Whenever you use your pasta machine to condition clay, always place the folded sheets so that the fold rests on the rollers or the fold is perpendicular to the rollers, then roll through. In this way, you will not introduce air pockets into the clay.

Stiffer clays, such as Kato Polyclay and Fimo Soft, may require a slightly different approach. Here are the steps.

1 Stand the bar of polymer clay upright and cut through to make two thick slices of clay.

2 Using an acrylic rod, roll the clay out to about ³/₈ inch. (I stand up when I flatten the slices, to apply more pressure on the clay. Press down firmly as you roll with the rod.) This "precompression" with the acrylic rod is important, because it minimizes crumbling and shredding of the clay.

3 After rolling, put the flattened sheets through the thickest setting of your pasta machine. To speed up the process, I reset the machine to a thinner setting and roll the sheet through again. At this thinner setting, I finish by folding and rolling the sheet as many times as needed to make the clay soft and pliable. The surface of the clay should have a soft sheen.

When conditioning many colors of clay, begin by working with the lightest color first, than move on to the darker colors. Many people ask why, when they roll clay through the machine, dark streaks sometimes appear. These streaks are caused by a chemical reaction between the nickel plating on the rollers and the clay. The Makin's Clay pasta machine, with its nonstick rollers, does not create streaks on sheets of clay.

If you do not have a food processor (for extremely dry or very old clay) or pasta machine, clays may be conditioned by hand by cutting the block into pieces, kneading each piece, then kneading the pieces together.

ROLLING SHEETS OF CLAY

When conditioning clay with a pasta machine, you end up with a sheet of clay. In your canework, you will need uniformly thick or thin sheets. For thin sheets, if you wish to roll thin sheets, do not force the clay immediately from setting 1 (thickest) to setting 9 (thinnest). Instead, roll the clay through setting 1, 3, 5, 6, 7, 8, and finally number 9. Do not skip settings above setting 5, as doing so might lead to clay shredding, wrinkling, or tearing.

As you work, hold the clay above the rollers, maintaining tension in the sheet as you roll through. If you find that the clay still shreds, try cleaning the plates beneath the rollers by rubbing an alcohol wipe back and forth until all collected clay is gone. If the machine is exceptionally clogged with clay between the rollers and the bottom plates of the machine, gently dislodge the clay with a bamboo skewer. If the clay still tears and shreds, the problem might be that the edge of a lower plate has been damaged or nicked. If the plates have been damaged, replacement plates may be available.

To create a sheet of greater thickness than the thickest setting of the machine, simply roll two sheets and press them together beginning at one edge and working toward the other, pressing air pockets from between the sheets as you work.

If you do not have a pasta machine, roll your sheets with an acrylic brayer or rod. First flatten the conditioned clay by hand. For thick sheets, select two magazines of the same thickness. Place the magazines on your work surface, spines facing, with a space between. Place the clay between the spines of the magazines and roll over the clay with the acrylic rod or brayer. For thinner sheets, try using Popsicle-type craft sticks in place of the magazines, or use the Pro Clay Roller with gaskets, from Prairie Craft. This 12-inch-wide acrylic rod comes with three pairs of gaskets of various diameters. Slide a gasket on each end of the rod and roll to produce sheets of even thickness.

BULLSEYE CANE

DONNA KATO
These two pins feature simple bullseye canes and simple stripe canes. Thick-gauge wire holds the three elements securely.

READY TO START experimenting with millefiori? Start here, with a basic bullseye cane. This simple cane is the foundation for many others, including the windowpane cane, the stained-glass cane, and the lace cane. After making a few bullseye canes and getting the technique down, you may wish to wrap more sheets around your cane to get more interesting effects.

1 Using your hands, roll a cylinder of one color. Make a sheet of another color. Wrap the cylinder with the sheet.

2 The easiest way to determine the correct place to cut the sheet is to roll the wrapped cylinder over until the leading edge touches the wrap sheet. Unroll, and you will see the mark made by the leading edge. Cut the sheet at that point and reroll.

3 Roll the cane to smooth the sides of the cylinder and join the seam of the wrap clay.

4 I wrapped the basic bullseye with a sheet of green. You need not stop here—more layers might be wrapped around for different looks.

5 Bullseye canes are limited only by your imagination! Experiment with color, shapes, and size to find your favorites.

1　　2　　3　　4　　5

REDUCTION

REDUCTION IS THE PROCESS by which you can miniaturize the diameter of your canes, shrinking the image contained in the cane. Some artists recommend squeezing the center of the cane and slowly moving out to the ends. I find that when I use this method, clay tends to splay out at the ends of the cane, resulting in greater waste. Reduction always involves waste, but it can be minimized.

To reduce a cane, whether it is round, square, or triangular, I prefer to reduce the ends of the cane, pinching them, then rolling the center out to catch up with the pinched ends. For this procedure, the clay must be softened throughout. This method minimizes waste at the end of the canes.

When reducing a large cane, press the ends of the cane to acrylic disks. The disks "grab" the clay, and this encourages the center of the cane to stretch out evenly. If you have very large canes, you might find that whacking the sides and top with a rod or slamming the center of the cane against your work surface helps activate the clay. Basically, do what you must to soften the center of the cane.

The best reduction occurs when the clay is soft throughout the cane. If the clay is not soft throughout, you may end up cracking or splitting the cane as you try to reduce it. Polymer clay responds to pressure, heat, and movement (twisting and sometimes compressing from the ends).

DONNA KATO
This three-cabochon pin uses translucent-set dot canes over metal leaf, plus strips cut from a striped slice.

TIP

Repeated slamming, used by many polymer clay artists to soften their canes, causes jolting to your hands and wrists that could lead to physical problems down the road. Take care! For this reason and because of the difficulties of reducing large canes, I make my canes small. Production caners have little choice in the matter, but most of us need not make massive canes.

There are those who rest their completed canes before reducing them. In my experience and with my clay, I find this only makes the reduction process more difficult. What works for one may not work for another; find what works best for you. The only hard-and-fast rule of reduction is that you must always work all sides of the cane, rotating round canes or flipping to the next side in reducing square and triangle-shaped canes.

REDUCING A ROUND CANE

Round canes are the simplest to reduce. Simply squeeze and rotate the clay until it softens and begins to move. Once the clay is moving, the cane may be placed on your work surface and rolled to and fro to smooth the surface and continue the reduction. When the clay is soft through and through, you may even gently pull the ends to stretch out the cane. Roll, stretch, roll, stretch!

1 Here is a round kaleidoscope cane wrapped in stripes. To reduce the cane, use basic techniques. Begin by grasping and lightly squeezing the cane in the palm of your hand. Rotate and squeeze until the cane is soft throughout.

2 Pinch down one end of the cane as you look at the cane end. Pinch the other end in the same fashion.

3 Here is a picture of the cane with pinched-down ends. With each reduction of the cane, I pinch the ends in the same way.

4 Place the cane on your work surface and roll down the center until it is the same diameter as the ends. The cane slice here shows the minimal waste at the end. If you wish to reduce the cane further, repeat steps 3 and 4.

REDUCING A SQUARE CANE

Reducing a square cane is a simple process. Here is a square cane, large for me!

1 Begin by squeezing the cane between your palms as shown. Turn the cane 90 degrees and squeeze the other two sides of the cane. Repeat until you feel the cane soften inside.

2 You can also place the cane on your work surface and push with your palm. Rotate the cane to press the next side. Continue rotating and pressing.

3 With your fingers, pull out and refine the corners of the cane every so often.

4 Continue pressing the sides of the cane and refining the corners. When the cane is approximately twice its original length, roll each side with an acrylic rod to smooth the sides.

5 Grasp the ends of the cane and twist back and forth—this twisting motion is very effective in cane reduction. Twist and gently stretch the cane.

6 Periodically lay the cane on your work surface and, holding one end, stroke each side of the length of the cane with your flat fingers, as shown in the picture. Flip the cane to the other end and repeat. You may also pick up the cane, hold one end (the cane will be dangling loose), and stroke two sides with your fingers in the same way potters pull their handles.

7 Repeat these steps until the cane is reduced to the desired size. As you reduce the cane, try to make sure that the cane is of uniform size throughout its length. If it is thinner in areas, thin the adjacent cane (pick it up and gently stretch, or hold and stroke) to match the thin parts. Here is a picture of the original cane, a reduced piece, and a four-dot cane made by dividing and reassembling the reduced piece.

REDUCING TRIANGLE CANES

Reducing a triangle cane is similar to reducing a square cane.

1 Begin by squeezing the sides of the cane gently to soften the interior of the cane. Here you see I am holding the cane and applying pressure to the three sides at the same time. You could also place the cane on your work surface and press two sides of the cane, then flip the cane to the next side, press two sides, flip, and so on.

2 When the interior of the cane is soft, place the cane on your work surface and gently pull the corners of the cane. Continue pulling gently on all corners to stretch out the cane.

3 Grasp the ends of the cane and twist back and forth. Once again, twisting the cane is most effective.

4 Gently stretch and twist the cane. If the cane does not stretch uniformly, so that there are parts that are thicker than others, place the cane on your work surface and even it up by stretching the thick parts to match the thin. When the cane is even, and good and soft, begin reducing the cane further by stroking its length. Place one finger on one side of the cane and your thumb on the other. Grasp one end of the cane with your other hand. As you stroke the two sides of the cane, concentrate your movement on the place where the cane meets your work surface. If you stroke the cane in the middle, you will create indentations. Flip the cane to the next side and repeat; flip and stroke. Flip the cane over to the other end and repeat. Continue working the cane from both ends until the cane is reduced to the size you want.

5 Here are the original cane slice, a reduced slice, and the kaleidoscope cane made from the reduced cane. As you can see, by concentrating the corners when stroking the cane, I was able to make them quite sharp.

Odd-shaped canes may also be reduced. This particular method of reduction requires some experience and that the clay be well conditioned and soft. So, it is best to reduce these canes immediately after making them. Gently grasp the cane ends, twist, and slowly pull apart. Twist and pull until the cane is the size you want. Some canes may be reduced in the conventional manner, then details restored by indenting the length of the cane with a needle tool.

OVERPACKING AND CUTTING CANE SHAPES

FOR SOME PROJECTS, you will want to place a round element within a cane of another shape. The easiest way to do this is with overpacking and cutting, which produces perfectly shaped canes. In this example, the goal is to make a square cane with an orange ring in the center. The "doughnut" (or bullseye) in the middle was made by wrapping a black cylinder with a thin sheet of white, then a thick sheet of orange (made by wrapping two thick sheets around the core), then a thin sheet of white again. Around this, three thick sheets of black clay were wrapped. To ensure the most accurate cutting, I recommend a thick, not thin, blade. Here are the steps for getting that nice, even square cane.

1 With a blade, mark the face of the cane with a square. The ring should be centered within the square. As you can see from this picture, where the corners should be there is no clay.

2 Cut four strips from a thick sheet of black clay and press them to the blank corners of the square. Now the corners are filled. Re-mark the square with the blade.

3 From a corner, mark the length of the cane with the blade. Repeat, marking an adjacent corner to make guidelines on the side of the cane. (For other shapes, use a cutter to mark your guidelines.)

4 Following the guidelines, slowly cut down the length of the cane, rocking the blade down one line, then the other, working slowly down the cane until you have cut to your work surface. Remove the excess clay. (This is a method employed by artist Sandra McCaw.) Repeat, marking an adjacent corner.

5 Continue cutting until you have a square. Turn the cane over to make certain that the ring is centered on the other end. Trim, if necessary. Now you have made your square cane. This method of overpacking, then cutting, may also be employed to make round, oval, rectangular, and triangular canes. Simply center the image, then press a cutter on the face of an overpacked cane. Following the impressed line, cut the excess clay away until the cane is round, oval, rectangular, or tringular in shape.

EMBEDDING CANE SLICES

EMBEDDING YOUR CANE SLICES right into the clay or using them as onlay elements is your choice and will depend on the particular piece you are making. If you are embedding, the goal is to smooth a cane slice into clay without substantially changing the size and shape of the original slice, and to embed so that you cannot feel the edges of the cane slice at all.

The thinner the slice, the more true to the original cane it will be. Thick slices will move and distort more when smoothed into background sheets—as you roll the cane to level the slice with the background, some of the cane slice will embed itself into the background, but most of it will move across the sheet surface. For this reason, you also want your background clay to be close to the same softness as the clay slice. A soft cane slice applied to a stiff background will move more across the background surface and will resist embedding into the background clay. On the other hand, a stiff clay slice applied to a soft background will do the reverse: It will embed itself into the background with minimal movement across the background, but you may not be able to easily remove the line created by the edge of the slice itself. There may be a time when you find these working characteristics useful in your work, but as a general rule, the clays used should be the same consistency for the most satisfying end result.

The first thing you must master is slicing your canes thin. Once you have cut the thin slices, place them on the clay lightly, then secure them by gently pressing from the center out. Here is the method I employ to secure a round cane slice.

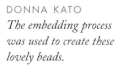

DONNA KATO
The embedding process was used to create these lovely beads.

1 Cut a thin slice from a round cane. (In this case I am using a jellyroll cane.) As you can see, the cane became somewhat distorted. With your fingers, gently coax the edge to make the cane round.

2 Place the cane on the clay surface—here a raw clay bead. Secure the center first.

3 Press the perimeter of the slice to the bead. I usually press north and south, then east and west, then the areas in between.

4 With a rod, roll the entire perimeter of the cane to the raw bead. Then roll the center of the cane out in all directions. The clay will respond to the direction you are rolling. In other words, if you roll from the center out, you will push the pattern out. If you roll from the outside in, you will push the pattern in. By employing both styles— rolling out *and* rolling in—you can control the way the pattern moves.

5 With your rod, roll the center of the cane out in all directions. Here is the finished piece.

CUTTING CANES

Many canes are made by dividing an existing pattern cane, then reassembling the parts in a new way. For these canes, and for canes made by overpacking, when cutting, you'll want to make certain that the cut is exact. Using a thick slicing blade will help prevent the clay from grabbing and torquing as you cut.

When cutting thin slices from assembled canes, you can use a thick or a thin blade. The thin blades cut cleanly through small canes, while thick blades are more rigid and so work better with larger canes. Wipe the blade with ArmorAll or water to prevent clay from sticking.

When using cane slices, slice as thinly and uniformly as possible. (Thick, uniform slices can be used, but you must fill any spaces between the slices with more clay). I cut slowly through my canes, watching the blade position as I cut, because it is possible to make minor adjustments along the way. Most of the time my goal is to cut very thin cane slices.

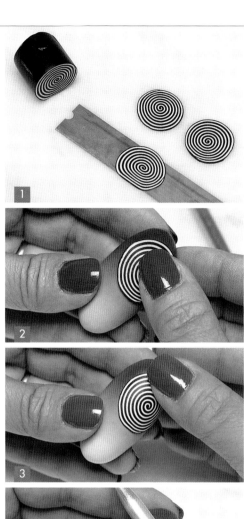

CREATING WITH MILLEFIORI

You have your tools and your materials. You've mastered some basic techniques you need. Now it's time to try some basic canes. In the last section, we started with the most basic cane of all: the bullseye cane, a simple round cane. Many canes are variations on the basic bullseye or the basic jellyroll cane, and as you work you will start to see the similarities between different types of canes. I hope you will enjoy making the projects in this section and that, like the best polymer clay artists, you will use the skills you are learning to create more and more innovative and personal work.

BASIC STRIPED SLAB

BASIC STRIPED SLABS can be combined with millefiori canes to produce countless new effects. Striped slabs, which are sometimes called striped-slab canes, are used in many projects. The pasta machine is a must-have for neat, even stripes. You can vary the effect by alternating thicker and thinner slices.

1 To make a basic striped slab, condition two colors of clay and roll them each through the same thickness of the pasta machine. Place one sheet on top of the other and trim the four sides.

2 If you wish to maintain the thickness of the layers as they are, finish by cutting the sheet in half and placing one half atop the other. For a slab with thinner stripes, roll the sheet through the pasta machine again. Finish by dividing and stacking two times to form a slab. Trim the four sides to even up the slab.

1

2

ABOVE: LESLIE BLACKFORD
Leslie's animals are always well dressed! This froggy fellow sports a suit made from a simple striped slab.

LEFT: LYNNE DE NIO
For this lovely choker, Lynne started with a fabric swatch, then duplicated the pattern in cane form.

Cactus Flower Pin

**TO MAKE ONE PIN,
YOU WILL NEED:**

Clay

Pasta machine

Acrylic rod

Blade

Fine double-pointed
  knitting needle or
  mandrel

Thick wire (16 gauge
  or 18 gauge)

Thin wire (20 gauge or
  22 gauge)

Needle tool

Clay extruder such as
  Makin's Clay
  Extruder (optional)

Small round cutter,
  slightly larger than
  the tie-tack back

Deli paper

Scalpel or X-Acto-type
  craft knife

Fine-grit sanding block

Fine metal file

2 tie tacks

Cyanoacrylate glue
  such as Kato
  Polyglue

THIS PRETTY, UNUSUAL PIN is a great way to use the techniques you are learning. The pin is not hollow, so it is on the heavy side. The best finding to use is not one pin back but two tie-tack findings, one secured to the back of the flower and the other at the base of the piece. I used Skinner Blends to make my pin, but you can use single-color clay for the petals and leaves if you like. Or learn how to make Skinner Blends (page 107.)

1 For the following striped slabs: thin stripes—a black-and-white slab and a deep green (green and black mixed) and a black, gold, and crimson (one part ultra blue and twenty parts red) slab. Thick stripes—make a lime green (yellow with a bit of green and a smaller bit of red) and pale lime green (white with a bit of lime green) slab. For the flower petals and leaves: Make a Skinner Blend plug approximately ¾ inch tall. Mine was made with a deep crimson (red with a bit of ultra blue), blended to pale yellow (white with a pinch of yellow). For the flower leaves: Make a Skinner Blend plug approximately ¾ inch tall of green and yellow. Or use solid colors for these elements. For the flower petals: Roll a snake of scrap clay 1 inch in diameter and 2 inches long. Wrap it with a thin sheet of white and reduce to 4 inches. The diameter should be ⁵⁄₁₆ inch. Cut a slice from the Skinner Blend flower plug, flatten it with your acrylic rod, then roll it through the thickest setting of the pasta machine. Reset the machine several times and roll through each time until the slice is a very thin strip. Trim the edge. Wrap the strip around the snake.

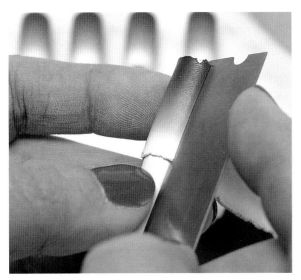

2 Trim the wrapped strip neatly to make a butt joint (no overlapping). Roll the piece on your work surface until the seam is joined. Cut segment. To cover exposed scrap clay, grasp the cylinder with the thumb and first finger and gently depress the ends. Working one end at a time, draw the clay from the sides up and over the scrap ends, rotating as you go. If any of the core is still showing, press it in with a pointed but blunt tool, such as a large-gauge knitting needle, then smooth the clay over to cover. Refine each end to form an almond shape. Repeat, making five almond-shaped petals.

3 For the stem: On a fine knitting needle or mandrel, place a cylinder of scrap clay. As if you were making a tube bead, pinch the ends and roll it out until it is about ³⁄₁₆ inch in diameter. Cut a ¼-inch-thick slice from the black-and-white striped slab. Roll the slice through the pasta machine, resetting and rolling until it is very thin. Cut the leading edge. Wrap the strip around the cylinder, cutting neatly to make a butt joint. Repeat, wrapping the cylinder with the black-and-white stripes. Roll to join seams. Cut a section 1½ inches long. Remove from the needle and slide onto a thick-gauge piece of wire.

4 Gather the flower petals and arrange them on your work surface. My piece has two petals in the back row and three in the front. Pinch the bottoms of the petals together.

5 With a needle tool, drill into one of the petals in the back row. Insert the stem wire. Slide the striped stem up to the flower, making sure they are in contact.

6 For the flower base: Cut a slice from the deep green and black striped slab. Thin the slice with the pasta machine. Wrap it around a cylinder approximately ¼ inch in diameter, just as you wrapped the black-and-white stripe around the clay to make the stem (do not use wire). Wrap the cylinder several times. Roll to smooth seams. Lay the piece straight on your work surface and cut it in half, dividing its width. Pick up one piece and wrap it around the base of the flower petals.

7 Extrude fine black snakes from a clay gun (I recommend the Makin's Clay Extruder). Pick up one snake and wrap it around the base of the flower petals. Wrap a second snake around.

8 Press the flower to your work surface to flatten the wrapped piece you wrapped around the base of the flower petals. This is where one of the tie tacks will be glued, and it is much easier to flatten it at this point.

9 Roll a medium-thin sheet of black clay. With a cutter, cut a disk close to the same diameter as the tie-tack base—it's better to make this a bit larger than the finding. Press the disk to the flattened piece. Nest the flower in baking soda, and bake at 300°F for 10 minutes.

10 For the leaves: Roll a large, almond-shaped form with scrap clay. Cut in half as if you were making a cabochon. Smooth the sides of the form by rolling with your acrylic rod. Wrap the upper quarter of the cabochon with a thin sheet of black clay to cover scrap clay. When the flower is cool, place it on a piece of deli paper and push the almond-shaped cabochon over some of the stem and the wire. Push the scrap clay around the stem and force the clay down to the paper, as shown in the picture. Then peel the paper from the clay.

11 The leaves are made in the same way as the petals. Use green clay or a slice from the green and yellow plug. Once the petals are formed, insert a thin wire and flatten them. Cut strips from the lime green and pale lime green striped slab. Thin them with the pasta machine. Starting at the top, wrap the stripes around the form. Trim away the excess at the top and the sides, as shown in the picture. Repeat to cover the entire form. Smooth with acrylic rod. Insert the wired leaves next to the stem, pushing the end of the leaf into the raw clay. Curve leaves.

12 Trim bottom with a Nublade to make it flat.

13 Roll a snake of scrap clay ¼ inch in diameter. Wrap it with a thinned strip cut from the crimson-and-gold striped slab. Cut the covered snake in half, and wrap one half around the base of the leaves. Trim excess. Bake for 10 minutes at 350°F.

14 For the backing: When the piece is cool, fill in any voids in the back with raw clay. (You might find a void next to the embedded stem, for instance.) Roll a medium-thin sheet of black clay and place it on a piece of deli paper. Cut a straight edge. Place the flower pin on the black clay, aligning the straight-cut edge with the top of the "collar" you made in step 13. With a scalpel, cut the black clay around the piece, as shown in the picture. For the final curing, wrap the flower with damp paper toweling to prevent any possible color shift. Bake at 300°F for 15 minutes.

15 Sand the back and the striped front of the piece with a fine-grit sanding block. "Clean up" flowers and leaves by filing with a fine metal file. Glue one tie tack to the black disk in back of the flower and the other near the bottom of the piece.

THIS SIMPLE IMITATION BONE is made in the same way as the Basic Striped Slab. Combining white clay and translucent clay produces a slab with the off-white color of bone.

1 Condition and roll a sheet of white clay and a sheet of translucent clay through the thickest setting of the pasta machine.

2 Place one sheet atop the other and trim the four sides. Roll the new sheet through the pasta machine, still set on the thickest setting.

3 Cut this striped sheet in half, place one half atop the other, and roll through again. Every time the sheet is divided, stacked, and rolled through, the layers will become thinner and thinner. Repeat two more times.

4 Cut the sheet in half and place one half atop the other. Repeat two more times to make a thick block. Trim the four sides.

DONNA KATO
This faux bone necklace is made from striped slabs and bullseye dots. The pieces were antiqued with oil paint.

ADDING A STRIPED BORDER

A SIMPLE STRIPED EDGE on a cane creates visual interest. Here's how you would add stripes to a simple bullseye cane.

1 Make a striped slab and a round cane. On the surface of the striped slab, press the 3mm side of a Marxit onto one solid-colored side of the slab. If you do not have a Marxit, use a ruler to measure and mark. Cut a slice following the mark. Roll the slice through the thickest setting of the pasta machine. This will not substantially change the thickness of the slice, but it will even it out. In this picture you see the original marked slab, a cut slice (at left), and another slice that has been rolled through the pasta machine (at right). As you wrap, cut and roll slices as necessary.

2 Secure one edge of a slice to the round cane. Lightly press to make sure that the slice is firmly in contact with the cane.

3 Add another slice, making sure that you alternate the stripe colors. Press the edges of the slices together. Then press the rest of the slice to the round cane.

4 Here is the covered cane. In this case, I needed four slices, and they fit almost perfectly. If they do not fit perfectly, you will have to slice and cut excess clay off the striped piece.

5 Roll the wrapped cane on your work surface to join the edges of the slices together. The finished cane should look smooth and finished, and a slice cut from it should have even stripes all the way around.

WINDOWPANE CANE

THE WINDOWPANE CANE is made of several bullseye canes, put together for a distinctive windowlike look. This technique, grouping canes together to create an entirely new cane, is important for the complex canes we will be making later.

1 Make a bullseye cane. The one shown here is translucent, wrapped with white, then black.

2 Reshape the cane to a square shape. This reshaping eliminates air pockets that might occur if you simply pressed the round canes together.

3 Reduce this cane so that it is at least 12 inches long. Cut into four pieces of equal length.

4 Reassemble the four pieces to make a square windowpane cane. The corners should meet, and the black lines should appear uninterrupted.

DONNA KATO
Two bright pendants spotlight windowpane canes.

ZIPPER CANE

ZIPPER CANES look a little like zippers with intermeshed teeth. They add a cheerful striped effect to the Pop Art Pin and other projects.

1 Begin by rolling a sheet of black clay through a thin setting of the pasta machine (I use setting 6). Cut the sheet in half. Roll a sheet of green clay through a medium setting of the pasta machine (I use setting 4). Stack up the three sheets up so the green sheet is in the middle, as shown in the picture. Roll this sheet through the pasta machine on the second thickest setting, then cut the sheet in half.

2 Mark the surface of a striped slab in 3mm increments, using a Marxit tool or a ruler. Cut the slices and roll each through the thickest setting of the pasta machine. Lay the slices made in step 1 on one half of the sheet. Roll with a knitting needle or an acrylic rod to join the slices together.

3 Press the other half on the striped side of the sheet. Roll with a knitting needle or acrylic rod to secure it. The completed cane is shown here.

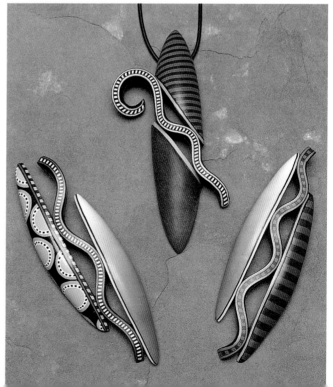

DONNA KATO
Three variations on the Pop Art Pin show how the techniques can be used to create different looks.

Pop Art Pin

THIS POP ART PIN uses the simplest of canes, plus a simple striped sheet cane. The key to a successful result is the accuracy of the simple dot cane (an over-packed windowpane cane, demonstrated on page 128), the carefully embedded cane slices, and finally, the finishing sanding that creates a smooth surface.

The pin made in the project appears at left. I've included the other two to show you different finishes. The one in the center shows what the piece would look like if I had buffed it to a high sheen. The piece on the right shows a different color scheme and a satin sheen, achieved by buffing against worn denim.

TO MAKE ONE PIN, YOU WILL NEED:

Clay

Pasta machine

Cutting blade

Thick knitting needle or brass tube

Needle tool

Scalpel or X-Acto-type craft knife

Kato Clear Medium

1 Here are the canes you will need, along with a sheet of green clay and the heart-shaped cabochon required to make this piece. The canes are two simple bullseye canes, a dot cane, and a zipper cane.

2 With the needle tool, scribe the line that will divide the dotted pattern from the green part of the piece. Cut slices from the dot cane, trying to cut them the same thickness (in this case, I do not cut them extremely thin). Starting at the tip of the heart, lay a slice on the cabochon. Pat down the sides lightly.

3 Trim the excess clay from the back of the cabochon and then, following the scribed line, cut and remove the excess cane from the front.

4 Pick up and position another cane slice, maintaining the dot pattern. Cut and remove the excess clay from the back. Continue, placing slices as needed and trimming from both the front and back of the piece.

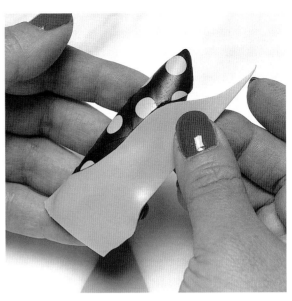

5 Roll the green clay through a setting that is approximately the same as the thickness of the cane slices. In my case, I rolled the clay through setting 7 of my pasta machine. With your blade, cut a curve that approximates the curve of the dot pattern on the piece.

6 Position and place the green sheet on the cabochon, adjusting as you go to match the curve.

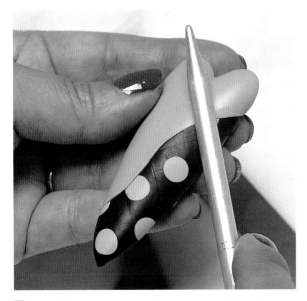

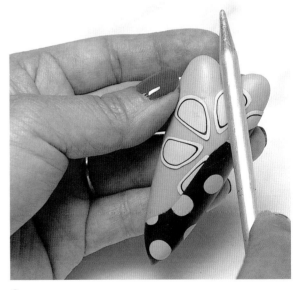

7 Smooth the entire piece with a knitting needle or brass tube, concentrating on where the cane slices meet and where the green sheet meets the caned part of the piece. When you are done with this step, everything should be joined and smooth.

8 In this picture, you can see the bullseye cane I selected for the petals. It was a bit large, so I reduced its size, then pinched along its length to create a petal shape. Cut thin slices and place them on the green clay. Trim the cane slices to conform to the curve. Roll the slices in, completely embedding them. You should be able to run your fingers across the surface of the piece and not feel any edges.

9 Cut a thin strip from the zipper cane. This piece should be thin, but not so thin that you can see through it to the pattern below. Lay this piece along the curve and press it in. Roll to completely embed the strip into the piece. (This is important— you don't want to sand away the zipper cane!)

10 Press the piece to a ceramic tile and bake for ten minutes at 300°F. When the piece is cured and cool, sand the front, beginning with 400-grit sandpaper. Follow up with 600-grit wet/dry sandpaper. (These coarse-grit papers will smooth the surface very quickly, but you must look at the piece constantly to make certain you do not sand away the patterns!) Sand the back with a coarse-grit sanding block until it is smooth. Because this pin is rather large, I have opted to use two tie tacks instead of a pin back. Glue two tie tacks onto the back of the piece as shown.

11 Roll a sheet of backing clay through a thin setting (I used setting 7). Place the sheet on a piece of deli paper. Press the prongs of the tie tacks into the clay. To improve the adhesion between cured and raw clay, apply a very light coat of Kato Clear Medium to the back of the piece.

12 Flip over the piece, remove the paper, and, using the holes made by the prongs to guide you, press the clay to the back of the piece and over the tie tacks.

13 With a blade, trim the excess clay from around the piece.

14 Here is the back of the pin before baking. I've also remembered to add my signature cane slice. Bake the piece for an additional ten minutes at 300°F. When curing a large, flat-backed pin such as this, I place two ceramic tiles in my oven and put the piece in face up so that the prongs of the tie tacks fall between the two tiles. The prongs hold the piece in position. Alternatively, embed the piece in a bed of baking soda for the curing.

ZIGZAG STRIPE PATTERN CANE

Zigzag canes are polymer clay pop art.

DONNA KATO
I covered a rock to make this odd little box featuring zigzag canes.

ZIGZAG STRIPE-PATTERN CANES perfectly illustrate several millefiori principles: division, reassembly, and reduction. These techniques can transform the simplest canes into complex patterns. Begin with a large striped slab. You may also make a version with two separate colored slabs, cutting each in half diagonally and then using only one half of each to make the cane.

1 Begin by making a basic striped slab. Trim the sides so that the face of the slab is square, or add alternating layers to make the face square. Stand the squared cane up on one end and slice down through on the diagonal. (Artist Sandra McCaw suggests "walking" the blade down from side to side.)

2 Separate the two halves. Press them together so that the stripes of one half are perpendicular to the stripes of the other and the newly formed shape is a right triangle.

3 Reduce this triangle to a total length of 4 inches. Trim the ends. Cut to divide this piece into two pieces of equal length. Reassemble the new pieces together in a mirror image.

4 Reduce this new cane to a total length of 4 inches. Trim the ends. Cut to divide this piece into two pieces of equal length. Reassemble as shown.

5 Cut this piece in two and press the sides together as shown to form a V.

6 Reduce this to a total length of 8 inches. Trim the ends. Cut in half and place the pieces side by side, forming a single zigzag.

7 Cut the cane in half again and place one half atop the other to form a double zigzag.

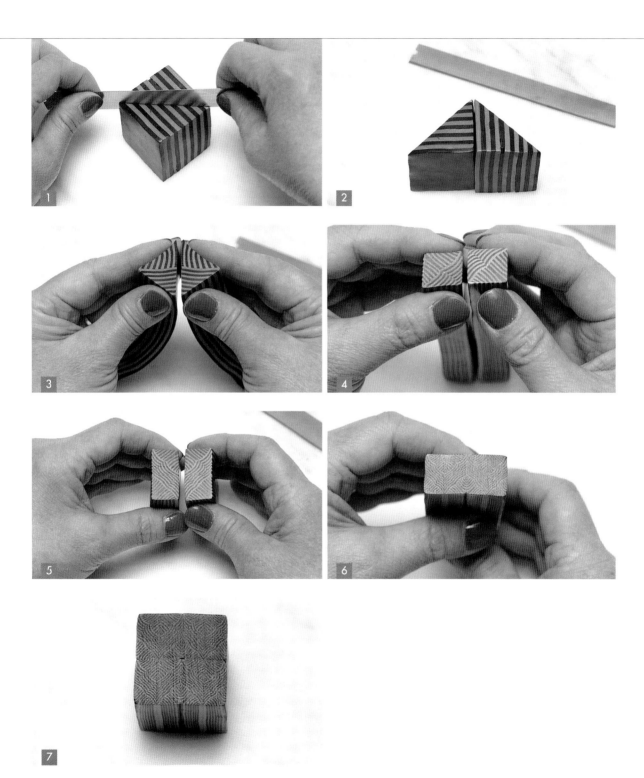

JELLYROLL CANE

THE JELLYROLL CANE, or balanced jellyroll cane, is used again and again in millefiori work. The shape is similar to a baked jellyroll cake, with soft cake rolled around a jelly filling. Jellyroll canes can have more "cake" or more "filling" to create visual variations. A balanced jellyroll like this one has about the same amount of cake and filling.

1 Begin by choosing and conditioning two colors of clay for your jellyroll cane. Roll each of the conditioned clays separately through the thickest setting of the pasta machine. Place one sheet atop the other and trim the four edges, making a neat square or rectangle.

2 Roll this square through the thickest setting of the pasta machine again. If you wish to make a jellyroll cane with thin striping and many revolutions, reset the pasta machine to a thinner setting and roll through again.

3 Fold the sheet in half, dividing the length. Flatten the fold with your fingers, pushing any air pockets out of the fold. Trim the open edge with a blade, making a beveled cut. From the fold, roll up tightly to the end.

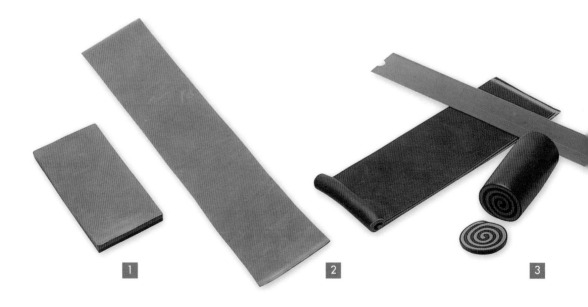

1   2   3

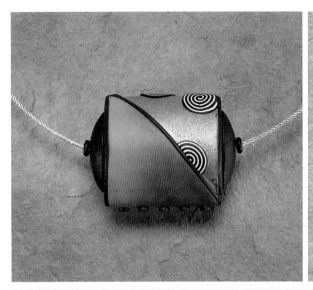

ABOVE LEFT: DONNA KATO
This pendant blends jellyroll slices and a Skinner Blend, both pressed to gold-painted black clay.

ABOVE RIGHT: DONNA KATO
Half of this pendant features gold and translucent jellyroll cane slices. Because of the mica, they shimmer.

LEFT: DANIEL TORRES MANCERA
Daniel is a multitalented artist working in silver and polymer clay. This silver ring is embellished with tiny jellyroll cane pieces.

TILE CANE

I'VE USED THIS CANE in my demonstrations for years. It illustrates how a very simple cane can be transformed into a complex pattern through division, reduction, and reassembly.

1 Make a balanced jellyroll cane. Trim the ends. Measure, then cut off a quarter of the length of the cane. Set this piece aside.

2 Stand the cane up on one end and cut through, dividing it in half. Rotate the cane 90 degrees and cut through again to form four wedges. Reduce the reserved piece from step 1 so that its diameter is about equal to the radius of the wedges. This reduced piece is now the center of the cane.

3 Place the round side of each of the wedges against the center piece. This piece is now roughly square.

4 Squeeze the opposing sides of the square together to expel air pockets and join the pieces. Roll each side with a brayer to smooth and sharpen the corners.

5 To create the tile pattern, reduce this new cane again, this time to twice its length. Cut the cane in half and place one half next to the other. Cut in half again and stack one half atop the other.

SNAIL-TYPE JELLYROLL CANE

THE SNAIL-TYPE JELLYROLL CANE looks more like a snail's shell than a balanced jellyroll does. To get the snail-like effect, choose clays with high contrast. Then make one sheet of clay much thinner than the other. When you roll your cane, the thin sheet will mimic the look of a snail's shell. Use these canes to add playful swirls to your pieces.

1 Condition two colors of clay. One color will be the primary color and the other will be the stripe; therefore, you will need to condition more of the primary color and less of the stripe. Roll the conditioned primary color clay through the thickest setting of the pasta machine. Trim the sides. Divide the sheet into three strips.

2 Using an acrylic rod, flatten one end of the stack, tapering it. Roll the stripe color through the thickest setting of the pasta machine. If you want your cane to feature a finer stripe, reset the pasta machine and roll the stripe-color clay through again to make a thinner sheet. If you wish to have a bold stripe through the cane, don't roll the sheet again. When your stripe sheet is ready, place the primary color stack atop the stripe sheet. Using a blade, trim all four sides. With a blade, bevel the edge opposite the tapering edge.

3 From the tapered end, roll the jellyroll up tightly. The clay should be soft and supple enough so that it will not crack as you roll. The finished cane displays the contrasting-color swirl.

DONNA KATO
These translucent black canes were placed and trimmed to fit exactly over crackled metal leaf.

CHECKERBOARD CANE

CHECKERBOARD CANES are fun. With their precise squares and sharp contrast, they offer countless eye-catching possibilities. Think of checkerboards (of course), racing flags, tiled floors. Less contrast in the colors will produce a more subtle effect, while high contrast sends the checkerboard message more forcefully.

1 Condition two colors of clay. Roll each sheet through the thickest setting of the pasta machine. Fold each sheet in half, pressing air from the folds of each sheet. Then place one folded sheet atop the other and trim the sides with a blade. Cut this stack in half and place one half atop the other.

2 From the stack, cut four slices, bearing in mind that each slice should be the same width as the height of one of the layers. You want each "cell" of your cane to be square. Note that the 5mm side of the Marxit is equal to two sheets rolled through the thickest setting of the pasta machine.

3 Separate the four slices and flip over every other slice. Then reassemble to make a checkerboard pattern.

4 Press the slices together, checking both ends to make certain that the pattern is in proper registration.

Simple quilt patterns can be made in much the same way as checkerboard canes.

1   2   3   4

Simple checkerboard rings race around a star-spangled heart.

Mira, known as Pinki, specializes in sculpture. Her animals are my favorites. This charming giraffe is covered with checkerboard canes and flowers.

CHECKERBOARD IKAT CANE

THE IKAT MILLEFIORI TECHNIQUE was introduced to the polymer clay community by Steven Ford and David Forlano. This cane has the distinct look of ikat fabric. Artists such as Kathy Amt and Susan Hyde have created their own ways to re-create the ikat effect in clay. Here's one of my versions of the theme.

1 Make a checkerboard cane, then squash the cane corner to corner with your fingers.

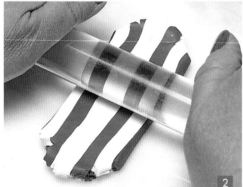

2 Roll the cane with an acrylic rod. Flatten it to make a strip just a bit thicker than the thickest setting of the pasta machine.

3 Roll the flattened strip through the thickest setting of the pasta machine.

4 Cut the strip in half and place one half atop the other, offsetting slightly, as shown in the picture. Note that offsetting at this point yields a tight zigzag pattern. To make a looser pattern, you could delay offsetting the pieces until you divide and stack to make the finished cane.

5 In this picture, you see the original piece from step 4 at left. The next slice has been rolled through the pasta machine again, cut in half, and stacked. The piece that is third from the left has been rolled through again and stacked. Further division and stacking made the finished cane, whose sides were trimmed.

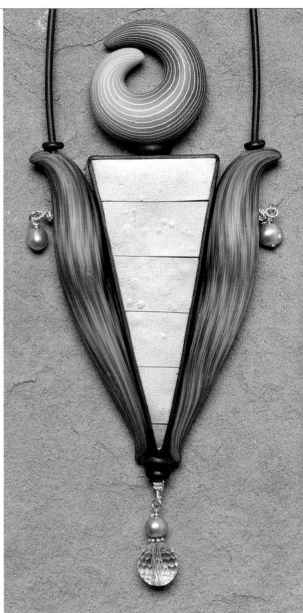

DONNA KATO

ABOVE LEFT: *These two pins feature checkerboard ikat canes.*

ABOVE RIGHT: *The sides of this pendant were made with a checkerboard ikat in green. The spiral on top was made from a Skinner Blend striped cane. The centerpiece is a plain clay triangle painted gold.*

LEFT: *This heart pendant is made from a basketweave cane that started as a checkerboard ikat cane.*

KALEIDOSCOPE CANES

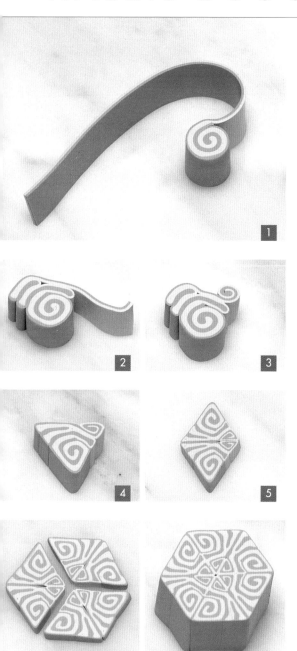

KALEIDOSCOPE CANES are simply complex canes made by reshaping a single cane into an equilateral triangle shape, reducing it, dividing it, and then pressing the six pieces together so that the adjacent sides mirror image one other. This process works with any cane you might have, or you can make a very simple version with this technique.

1 Condition two colors of clay and roll each through the thickest setting of the pasta machine to make a sheet. Place one sheet atop the other. Reset the machine to a medium setting and roll the two-color sheet through to make a long strip. Fold the strip in half and cut the edge opposite the fold. From the fold, start to roll up tightly (you are beginning with a balanced jellyroll). Do not roll up the entire piece.

2 Instead of rolling up all the way to make a balanced jellyroll, fold the sheet back and forth.

3 Finish by rolling the tail up into a small jellyroll. The longer the strip, the more you can fold, the more intricate the pattern becomes.

4 Force the cane into a triangle shape. To make a 2-inch-long finished cane composed of six repeated elements, reduce this triangle piece to approximately 12 inches.

5 Trim the ends of the cane, then cut the piece in half, dividing its length. Press the halves together so the pattern creates a mirror image. Experiment by turning the pieces and trying different sides of the pieces together to find the most pleasing pattern.

6 Cut this cane into three pieces of equal length. Press them together to create the whole cane.

7 Press all sides of the cane to expel air from between the separate parts. Here is the finished cane.

DONNA KATO
Here are some canes used to embellish beads (necklace, left). The necklace on the right illustrates the use of the simple sheet method for making kaleidoscope canes.

USE-WHAT-YOU-HAVE KALEIDOSCOPE CANES

Here is another method for making kaleidoscope canes. This technique is perfect for using up any odds and ends of canes and clay.

1 Roll a thin sheet of one color. In these pictures, I have used black. Cut the sheet into a long, thin rectangle. Onto this sheet place slices from striped canes, snakes of various colors, and even other canes. Cover the rectangle with these elements.

2 Trim the edge that you will begin rolling from. From this edge, roll up into a jellyroll.

3 Reshape the mass into an equilateral triangle. Reduce this piece to a length of 12 inches.

4 Trim the ends, then cut the piece in half, dividing the length. Press the pieces together so the two sides form mirror images of each other.

5 Cut this piece into three equal-length pieces and arrange them to make a six-sided whole cane.

6 Press the pieces together to expel air from between the separate parts.

7 Here you see the cane from step 6 reshaped and rolled to create a round kaleidoscope cane.

Dede's beads and jewelry are much in demand. These Delft blue pins show off her lovely canes.

This spear necklace features a kaleidoscope cane on one side.

KLIMT CANE

I CALL THIS TYPE OF CANE a Klimt cane because it resembles the patterns seen in the work of the painter Gustav Klimt. The basic technique—extrusion through a clay gun and exploiting the interesting ring pattern it creates—began with Esther Anderson, who showed it to me years ago. The best inexpensive, general-use clay gun I have found is made by Makin's Clay, but this technique will work with other clay guns as well.

1 Mix your color palette. Roll each color into a cylinder approximately the same diameter as the barrel of the clay gun you are using. Build a stacked cylinder by pressing a different color cylinder to a slice, then cutting. Press a new color cylinder to the last one; cut. Continue, building a multicolored stack. The arrangement should look random, so it works best to vary the contrast of the pieces.

2 Soften and roll the multicolored roll against your work surface—it is best for the clay to be soft and warm when you drop it into the clay gun.

3 Fit the clay gun with a square disk. Drop the warm clay into the barrel, then screw the top onto the clay gun.

4 Extrude the clay through the disk. If you find it difficult to extrude, try holding the barrel in a piece of rubber shelf liner for a better grip.

5 Cut the extruded clay in half and press the halves together. (I flip one piece over so the adjacent pieces are not identical.)

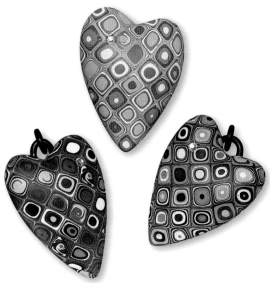

TOP: MEISHA BARBEE
Meisha's use of color, texture, and pattern create simple yet elegant pendants.

BOTTOM: DONNA KATO
The shapes and colors in these striking heart pendants remind me of paintings by the artist Gustav Klimt.

6 Cut this new piece in half, then press the halves together, flipping one half to the other end to mix up the cells.

7 Repeat two more times to form a large block, then roll the four sides with an acrylic rod.

8 Your Klimt cane is finished. Here is my version, in greens, yellows, blues, and a touch of copper.

Klimt Pyramid Ring

RINGS TAKE A LOT OF ABUSE, so use the strongest clay you possibly can. The ring form used in this project was made by Rio Grande and is meant for use with metal clays. You may use a metal cutter as a ring form, if you have one that fits your finger.

Note that the band of this ring is off-center. It was an accident but, due to the size of the pyramid, it actually makes the piece more comfortable because the band sits in the correct place on my finger without the pyramid sitting on a knuckle.

1 Condition and form a thick cube of scrap clay. With your blade, lightly impress a line from corner to corner, then score from the opposite corners to make an X.

2 Starting at the intersection of the two lines, make an angled cut to the base of one side of the cube. Repeat, cutting the four sides of the pyramid. My scrap clay contained some pearl clay. A little metallic clay mixed in will help you cut clean, as it sticks to the blade less.

3 Cut four thin slices of equal thickness from the Klimt Cane block. Place one slice of Klimt cane on one side of the pyramid. Turn it over, and with your blade, cut away the excess clay. Repeat, placing a slice on the next side of the pyramid.

4 Cover the remaining two sides of the pyramid in the same manner. Bake for 15 minutes. After the pyramid is cured, sand the sides and bottom of the pyramid.

5 Roll a *thin* sheet of black clay. Brush a light coat of Kato Clear Medium on the bottom of the pyramid. Place the clay on the bottom of the pyramid and, with a blade, trim around the four sides. Set aside. Onto the ceramic ring form, apply a coating of Repel Gel. Let the gel dry.

6 Roll a medium-thin sheet of black clay—mine was rolled through setting 5 on my Makin's machine. For comfort, the band of the ring should not be too thick or too wide. Cut a thin strip, about ¼ inch (7mm) wide, from the sheet of clay. Wrap it around the ring form, cutting away the excess to form a butt joint.

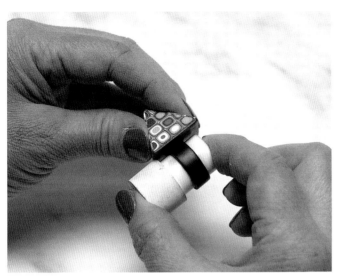

7 Position and press the pyramid onto the band of the ring, covering the butt joint. Push the ring into a bed of baking soda for support and bake for 30 minutes at 300°F. When cool, remove the ring from the form. Then lightly sand the band and the black clay on the bottom of the pyramid with 400-grit wet/dry sandpaper.

8 With soft black clay, fill in the space between the band and the bottom of the pyramid. Then, using a sculpture tool, press clay into the space between the band and the pyramid piece.

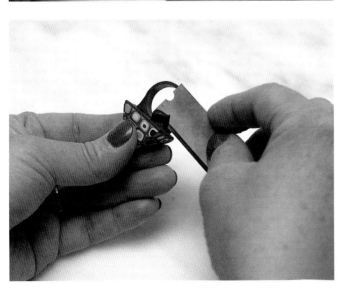

9 Finish by trimming three sides of the band with a blade so that the band meets the back of the pyramid neatly. Bake again in baking soda for 15 minutes at 300°F. When it is cool, sand the entire ring. In difficult to reach areas, use a file, then follow up with fine-grit sandpaper.

SHAPE-SHIFTING CANES

THESE CANES WERE DEVELOPED as a result of two things: first, because Sandra McCaw showed how she alters the appearance of canes by altering their overall shape; and second, because, at an artists' retreat, Shane Smith demonstrated what she had done using Sandra's shape-shifting. Sandra says she's "adding grace," and that's exactly what happens.

What I love about the canes I've made using the same principle is that there is no cane packing. You begin with one simple element. Try this technique with canes that you don't particularly care for—you might be pleasantly surprised by what happens.

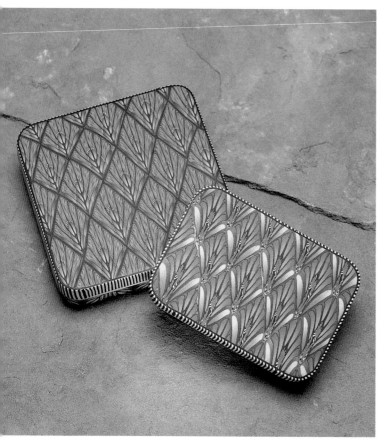

ABOVE: DONNA KATO
These two little boxes feature shape-shifting canes.

RIGHT: SANDRA McCAW
Sandra has used Skinner Blends to create arcing highlights, giving these earrings a three-dimensional appearance.

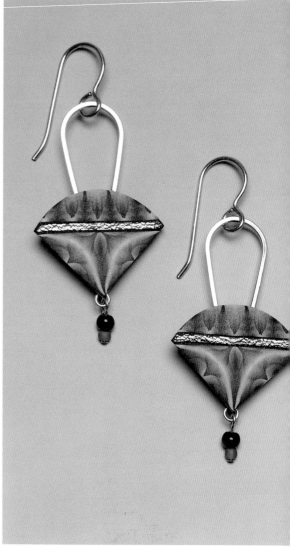

PATTERN 1

This technique starts with a simple bullseye cane and builds to create an intricate pattern. Use high-contrast colors so the pattern will stay clearly visible through all the steps.

1 Begin by making a large Skinner Blend bullseye cane (see page 119 for directions). Wrap it with a thin sheet of another color (I used black).

2 Wrap the cane with a sheet of what will be your background color, as shown in the picture. If the sheet is thick, more of the background will be shown; if it is thin, less of it will be apparent.

3 Reshape the bullseye into a capsule shape by flattening with an acrylic rod.

4 Reduce the slab and divide it into three pieces of equal length. Place them side by side and press them into a square. Refine by rolling each side with your rod.

5 Reduce the cane and divide it into four pieces of equal length. Then arrange the pieces in a basketweave pattern.

6 Push in the corners of the square, making the cane round. It will not be a perfect circle.

7 Bring the cane back to a square shape by pulling out what were the centers of the flat sides of the original square cane.

8 Reduce the cane further, cut it into four equal-length pieces, and reassemble them as shown.

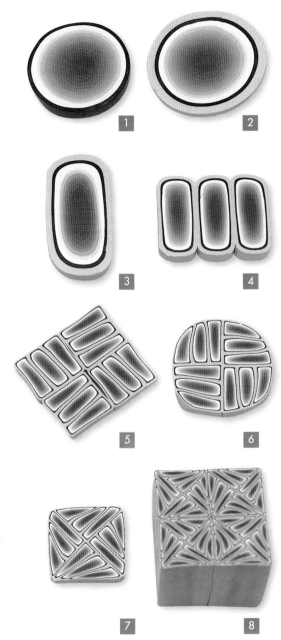

PATTERN 2

This pattern is made by reshaping a basic square-faced cane into a triangle-shaped component. The component can then be assembled to create different patterns. In this case, I've begun with a simple striped slab.

1 Make a striped slab. Trim it so that the face of the cane is square.

2 Place the cane on your work surface so that the stripes are perpendicular to the work surface. Push against one side of the cane, angling it as shown.

3 Force down the top edge so that the other side lies flat against your work surface. The square-faced cane is now triangle shaped. Reduce the cane to a length of 6 to 8 inches and divide it into two equal-length pieces.

4 Make a Skinner Blend bullseye cane (see page 119 for directions) and wrap it with a thin sheet of black. Force it into an almond shape.

5 Insert the almond-shaped bullseye between the pieces from step 3.

6 Press the triangle-shaped pieces around the center piece. The piece is now fan shaped.

7 To square it up, push the cane against your work surface and force it into a square shape.

8 Reduce the cane to a length of at least 8 inches. Trim the ends until the pattern looks good and divide the piece into four pieces of equal length. Press them together as shown in the finished cane.

PATTERN 3

This basic component cane is created in much the same manner as Pattern 2.

1 Begin with a Skinner Blend bullseye cane (see page 119 for directions) and wrap it with a medium-thick sheet of black.

2 Reduce the cane, then cut it into three pieces of equal length. Arrange the pieces side by side, then force them into a square shape.

3 As you did in Pattern 2, force the square cane into a triangle shape. Here are the intermediate and finished triangles.

4 Divide the triangle cane into two pieces of equal length, then press it together as shown.

5 Reduce this piece and divide it into four pieces of equal length. Notice that the arrangement of the four pieces in this cane is different; it looks more like a modified feather pattern.

STARRY NIGHT CANES

These canes are made from chopped-up clay.

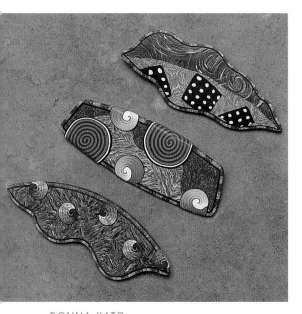

DONNA KATO
These three pins were made by combining Starry Night canes with dot, jellyroll, snail-type ikat jellyroll, and Starry Night swirl canes.

THIS CANE IS A WONDERFUL WAY to use any cane ends and miscellaneous bits and pieces of clay you might have on your work table. A food processor is a real help to make the chunks of clay, but if you don't have one, you may also use a knife or blade to chop the clay on your work surface by hand. The results remind me of the famous painting by Vincent van Gogh, *The Starry Night*, and so I named these canes in honor of it.

When you roll a double thickness of clay through the pasta machine, the clay widens a bit while it nearly doubles in length. You can choose from two different patterns in stacking the sheets. The side that runs perpendicular to the rollers will features long streaks, while the colors in the other side will have a choppier appearance. The decision to use one or the other when making the face of your canes is a matter of personal preference.

1 With a food processor or by hand with a blade, cut up and mix various colors and bits of clay into small chunks.

2 Process the clay in the processor until the clay is broken up into bits.

3 Form this mass into a slab and roll it with your acrylic rod. If the clay bits stick to the rod, place a sheet of deli paper on the slab, then roll.

4 Roll the sheet through the pasta machine on the thickest setting. Cut the rolled sheet in half and place one half atop the other, as shown in the picture. Roll the double sheet through again. The number of times you divide and roll through depends largely on the size of the bits you've cut or processed. The smaller they are, the fewer times you will divide, stack, and roll through. My piece was rolled through, then folded and rolled three more times.

5 After rolling through, cut the sheet in half and place one half atop the other. Trim the four sides. Inspect the sides, as they will look different: Some will feature long streaks and the others will have a choppy appearance. When you divide

and stack, make sure you maintain the same "grain" on the outer sides. Cut the slab in half again and stack one half atop the other. Trim the sides with a blade. If the face of the slab isn't square, reshape it with your fingers or cut sides until it is square. This basic square cane is the starting point for creating a Starry Night zigzag cane, a swirl cane, a tile cane, a basketweave cane, and many others. You can see the long streaks along one side and the choppy pattern on the other cane face.

STARRY NIGHT TILE CANE

1 Make a Starry Night slab, then cut the slab in half diagonally, as shown in the picture.

2 Separate the halves and reassemble as shown to make a triangle-shaped cane.

3 Reduce the triangle-shaped cane, then cut it in two equal-length pieces; remember to trim the ends. Press the two pieces together to make a mirror image and press to create a cane.

4 Reduce this cane to a length of approximately 8 to 10 inches. Trim the ends and divide the cane into two pieces of equal length. Press the halves together as shown and make a cane.

5 Cut this cane into two pieces of equal length and press them together.

6 The finished cane looks like this. Roll each side with an acrylic rod to even up and square the corners.

7 This large piece is made of four slices from the cane, placed side by side and rolled to join the seams.

STARRY NIGHT SWIRL CANE

I make this cane in both opaque and primarily translucent versions. By mixing translucent with opaque colors, you will be able to slice this cane thinly and apply the slices selectively over opaque slices, adding curved lines and a hint of color for additional interest.

1 Make a basic Starry Night slab. In this case, the face of the cane is made using the side, not the face, of the original slab.

2 Taper one end of the slab, Squashing the square end of the cane.

3 Roll a thin sheet of black or another color. Place the slab on the black sheet and trim all around. (This step is optional.)

4 Roll up tightly from the tapered edge. Work slowly, giving the thin sheet a chance to stretch without cracking.

5 A slice cut from the cane shows its colorful interior. I leave the ends raw, but you may opt to taper the end before rolling. The cane is rolled like the snail-type jellyroll on page 77.

DONNA KATO
This pin features Starry Night swirl cane slices, sanded and buffed.

1   2   3   4   5

STARRY NIGHT ZIGZAG CANE

The Starry Night zigzag cane is made exactly the same way as the zigzag cane (see page 72). The grain of the basic Starry Night slab should be regarded as the stripes in that cane.

The zigzag cane on the left was made using the long-grain side of a slab, while the center and right canes used the choppy sides of their slabs.

DONNA KATO
For these pieces, I used a combination of Starry Night canes. The light blue areas are Starry Night zigzag canes.

DONNA KATO
The frame of this pin is covered with slices from a Starry Night zigzag cane made with mostly metallic clays.

Starry Night Pin

THIS COLORFUL PIN uses Starry Night canes as a background for bold elements in the foreground. You could make endless variations on this basic idea, using the colors in your scrap canes to inspire a wide variety of projects. For the foreground colors, think about choosing shades that will coordinate with the clothing you plan to wear with the pin.

TO MAKE ONE PIN, YOU WILL NEED:

Clay

Pasta machine

Blade

Acrylic rod

Ceramic tile

Fine-grit sanding block

Kato Clear Medium

Scalpel or X-Acto-type craft knife

Pin back

Cyanoacrylate glue such as Kato Polyglue

Dish scrubbie for texturing back

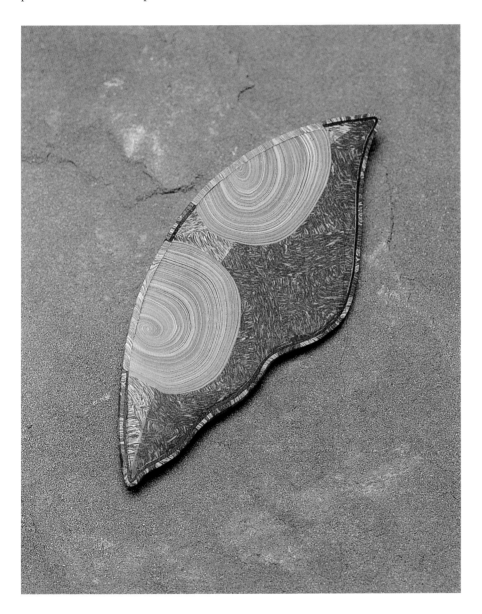

1 Make several Starry Night canes. Then, for the decorative sheets: Roll a medium-thick sheet of scrap clay. Onto the sheet, place a thin sheet of white. Roll the two-layer sheet to a medium-thin setting of the pasta machine (I use setting 5). Cut the sheet in half. From a square cane, cut thin slices and place them side by side on the white side of the trimmed sheet. Roll with a rod to smooth and join the cane seams. Roll this through a medium-thin setting of the pasta machine (I use setting 5). Following the same instructions, make a second decorated sheet.

2 Place the two sheets on a ceramic tile, overlapping one slightly over the other. With a blade, cut an arc through both sheets, as shown in the picture. Remove the excess clay from the top and bottom sheets, then butt them together at the cut. With your fingers, press the seam to join the two pieces together, then roll lightly with a rod.

3 With your scalpel, cut the shape of the pin.

4 Cut two thin slices from a Starry Night swirl cane. Place them on the pin, then roll the slices into the piece until they are completely embedded into the clay and you cannot feel them on the surface.

5 With a blade, recut the shape. On the ceramic tile, bake the piece for 10 minutes at 300°F. For the backing sheet: Roll a medium-thick sheet of scrap clay. When the piece is baked and cool, brush the back of the piece with Kato Clear Medium and press the backing sheet to the baked piece. Trim around with a blade or scalpel. Set aside.

6 For the striped edging: Roll a thin sheet of black (I use setting 8). Cut two slices from the same canes used to make the patterned sheets. Roll with an acrylic rod, then roll each slice through the pasta machine to a medium-thin thickness (I use setting 6). From one slice, with your blade, cut a thin strip. Lift it with your blade, position it on the black sheet, and press it in place. Cut a strip from the other slice, repeat, alternating the slices, as shown in the picture. After the slices have been placed, roll the sheet through the pasta machine to a medium-thin setting (I use setting 6). Roll the sheet through so that the stripes are perpendicular to the rollers of the machine.

7 Brush a light coat of Kato Clear Medium on the edge of the piece. Cut a slice from the Starry Night swirl cane. Roll it through the same medium-thin setting (I use setting 6). For the edging: Cut a strip from the thinned Starry Night swirl cane. Align it with the swirl pattern on the front of the piece. Trim it where the pattern changes from the swirl to the basic pattern.

8 Cut a strip from the striped edging sheet. Place this strip next to the swirl edging. Trim where the next swirl begins, as shown in the picture. Continue wrapping the appropriate edging around the entire piece. The object is to extend the surface swirl down along the edge of the piece.

9 With a blade, cut excess clay from the front of the piece. Turn over the piece and carefully trim away any excess edging clay. Bake the piece again for 10 minutes at 300°F.

10 For the invisible pin-back setting: When the piece is cool, sand the back flat. Around the perimeter of the piece, apply Kato Clear Medium. Do not put the medium in the center of the piece.

11 Roll a sheet of black clay through a thin setting (I use setting 8). Press the clay to the back of the piece. Trim around with a scalpel or blade. Then position the pin back on the black clay. Cut around the pin back with a scalpel. Lift the pin back and the cut-out clay.

12 Glue the pin back in the cutout. Set aside the cut-out piece of clay; you'll need it later. Compare the reserved cutout with the seated pin back. It is probably a bit too long, so cut it to the size that will fill the space, covering the glued down pin back, without interfering with the working mechanisms of the pin back itself. Press the cutout over the hole in which the pin back sits. Using a rolling tool, sculpture tool, or your fingers, smooth and flatten the clay to join the seams. Texture the entire back of the pin (I used a dish scrubbie). Bake this piece one last time for 15 minutes at 300°F. Finally, sand the front and sides of the piece with a fine-grit sanding block for a matte finish.

MILLEFIORI AND THE SKINNER BLEND

When Judith Skinner invented the Skinner Blend, I wonder if she realized how she would influence the work of so many polymer clay artists around the world! The Skinner Blend is a simple way to combine two colors of polymer clay into a single shaded blend. Making a three-part Skinner Blend is almost as easy. Incorporate Skinner Blends into your work to create beautiful shading and tints. The blends can suggest a sunset, a night sky, the ocean, a flower, or some part of a fantastic world that exists only in your own imagination.

TWO-PART SKINNER BLEND

KAREN SEXTON

Artist Karen Sexton has used shapes cut from Skinner Blend sheets to make this lovely pin, texturing the surface for greater visual interest.

THE MOST BASIC SKINNER BLEND is a seamless blend of two colors, so it is called a two-part Skinner Blend. This simple method for creating sheets of perfectly graded color is so easy . . . just be sure to follow the directions exactly. Then you can use your Skinner Blends to add rich, subtle shades to almost any project. Review the section on color on page 36, and try unusual color combinations that will surprise everyone who sees your work!

1 A simple two-color blend begins with two right-angle triangles, the same size and shape. After selecting and then conditioning the colors that you wish to blend, roll each color through the thickest setting of your pasta machine to make two sheets. Any time you roll continuously through the pasta machine, you end up with a more or less rectangular or square sheet, so for each sheet, grasp a "corner" of the sheet and fold it to its opposite "corner."

2 Place one folded sheet atop the other, matching the folded (diagonal) sides. With your Kato Nublade, make two cuts to create a neat 90-degree angle opposite the folded edges.

3 Separate the two triangles and reassemble them, butting the folds (diagonals) together to form an overall rectangle or square shape. Note that the corners do not meet, but tabs extend a bit, as shown. (If the corners met exactly, the sheet would be entirely graded and there would be no evidence of the original colors used in the blended sheet.)

4 The first time you roll the two-color sheet through the machine (on the thickest setting), make certain that your two colors physically touch the rollers. Then roll the sheet through. (If you are making a three-part Skinner Blend, make sure all three colors touch the rollers.)

5 Now fold the sheet so that the same color edge lies on the same color edge—that is, cream on cream edges and, on the opposite end, violet on violet. (Usually your folded sheet will be a long rectangle.) After the first time through the pasta machine, fold the sheet in this way each time you roll it through.

6 Place the fold on the rollers and roll the sheet through. Finish the blend in the same way—by folding the sheet again, same color edge on same color edge. There is no set number of times you must roll the sheet through the machine to make a streak-free Skinner Blend; the number depends on the opacity or translucency of the clay you are using. Translucent colors require fewer runs through the machine, as the translucent clay conceals streaking.

TIP

As easy as it is to make a Skinner Blend, it is also possible to roll the sheet through incorrectly. If you remember these simple instructions, you won't make that mistake.

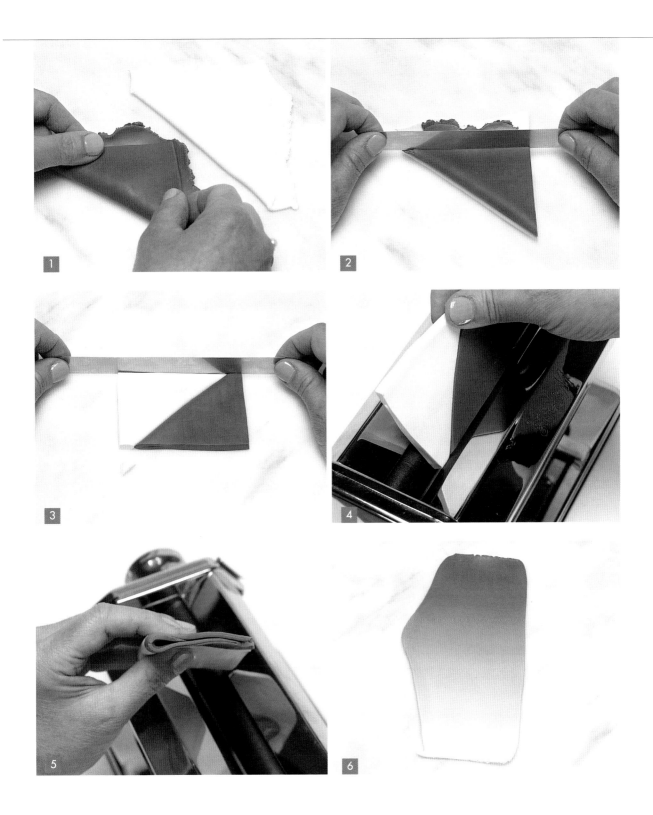

THREE-PART SKINNER BLEND

DONNA KATO
For this pendant, Skinner Blend waves were inserted into a Skinner Blend–covered pod.

SKINNER BLENDS of more than two colors are easy to create, almost as easy as two-part Skinner Blends. As with the two-part version, the colors on the ends are right-angle triangles. By volume, you will need twice the amount of clay in the center colors as you need on each end.

1 Choose your three colors and condition them. Then begin by making the end triangles, folding their respective sheets in half and folding the center color diagonally.

2 Place one sheet atop the other, matching the fold sides. By making two cuts, one creating the diagonal side of the triangle and another to form the 90-degree angle, you will cut the end colors the same shape and size, at the same time.

3 Place the center color piece on your work surface point down. Separate the cut end triangles. Place them on the center color as shown. Now you have established the shape of the center triangle.

4 Following the diagonal sides of the end color triangles, cut through the center color.

5 Separate the cut triangles, remove the excess center-color clay, and rearrange the pieces side by side, as shown.

6 As with the simple two-part blend, the first time you roll through the pasta machine, make certain that more than one color is physically touching the rollers. Then roll the sheet through. After that, fold the same color edge onto the same color edge, place the fold on the rollers, and roll through. Continue folding and rolling until the sheet is graded and streak free.

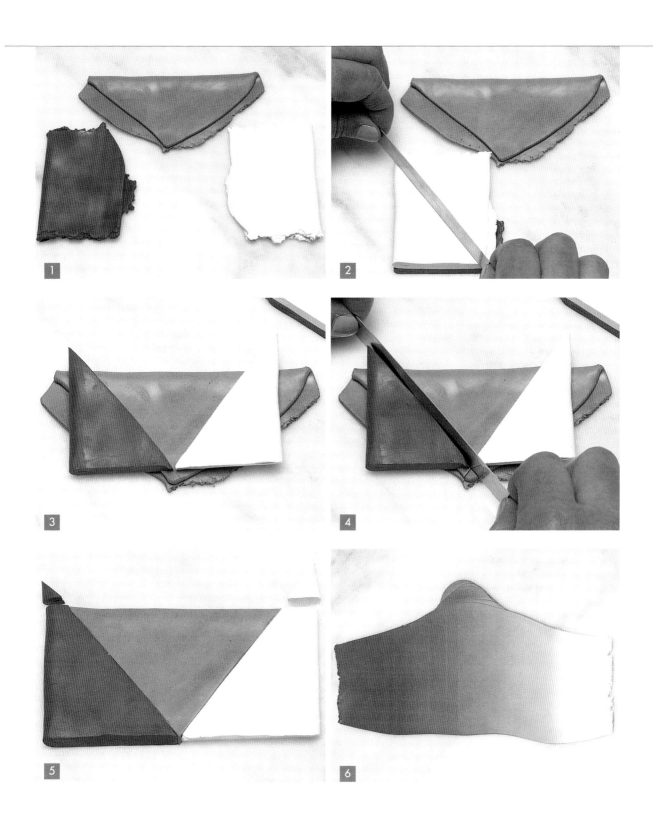

SKINNER BLEND PLUGS

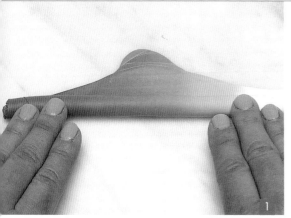

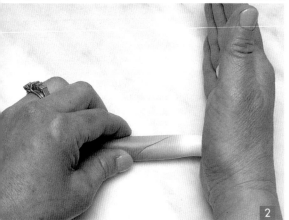

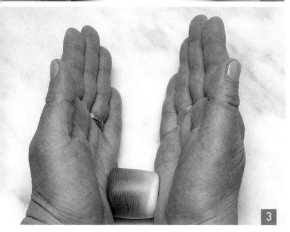

YEARS AGO, I made a piece to be used as part of the cover for a polymer clay calendar. I created a Skinner Blend rainbow sheet, and from it cut the letters to form the words on the calendar cover. What remained was a sheet with letter-shaped holes in it!

As I looked at this sheet, I just couldn't bear to mix it up, as most of it was perfectly usable. I decided that I'd save this blend. So I rolled up the sheet, rolling the same color onto itself. After rolling, I flattened the sheet, then rolled it through the pasta machine, folding and rolling to expel air from the clay.

At this point, I had a nice, even Skinner Blend sheet that I could have wrapped in plastic and kept for later use. But somehow I knew there was an even more space-saving, even more efficient way to store Skinner Blends than in sheets, so I decided to try to find it.

1 Roll up the Skinner Blend sheet, making it a Skinner Blend cigar.

2 To shorten the cigar, compress it using a sort of reverse reduction process, working the ends of the clay toward the middle.

3 After the reverse reduction was done, you will have a Skinner Blend plug, as shown in the picture. In this "condensed" form, Skinner Blend sheets may be stored compactly and transported easily. To turn a plug into a sheet, just flatten the plug, stretching it out side to side and top to bottom, then roll it through the pasta machine. Most often, though, I cut slices from the plugs for backgrounds on pendants, pins, and other items. This is the easiest way to create short Skinner Blend pieces.

Skinner Blend Tube Bead Eyeglass Leash

THESE COLORFUL TUBE BEADS are made with Skinner Blend plugs. It's a fact of life: We all need reading glasses as we get older. And then the big question becomes "Where are my glasses?" This cheerful eyeglass leash will keep those reading glasses close at hand, while making a very striking style statement. Personalize your eyeglass leash by using favorite colors, the colors of local sports teams or schools, or any other combination that appeals to you.

FOR ONE EYEGLASS LEASH, YOU WILL NEED:

Clay

Pasta machine

Blade

Needle tool

Fine knitting needle, skewer, or mandrel

Marxit or ruler

Small glass beads for spacing between polymer beads

Thread for stringing leash or monofilament (fishing line)

Eyeglass leash findings or two small rubber O rings

Lighter for securing monofilament

1 Roll a thick cylinder of white clay. (Notice that in this case, I do not use a scrap-clay core, because the core will be visible on the ends of each bead.) Pierce the center of the cylinder with a needle tool, then remove the tool and place the cylinder on a knitting needle or skewer the desired size of the finished hole. Then select the Skinner Blend plugs you want to use on your beads. Cut pieces from the Skinner Blend plugs and roll them through the thickest setting of the pasta machine. Roll a sheet of black clay through the same pasta-machine setting. I've also rolled a sheet of dull green through the same setting. Lay strips from the plugs and thin strips from the solid sheets on the cylinder until it is covered. Roll the cylinder to smooth and join the seams.

2 Pinch the ends of the clay to the knitting needle; this will prevent the ends from splaying out as you roll out the clay. Roll and twist the clay on the skewer. As you roll, the clay will move toward the ends and the diameter of the tube beads will decrease. As you can see, the clay has moved to the ends of the knitting needle and the diameter of the tube beads are too large. Cut off a segment by rolling the clay-covered knitting needle as you cut with the blade. Remove the long section and set it aside for later use.

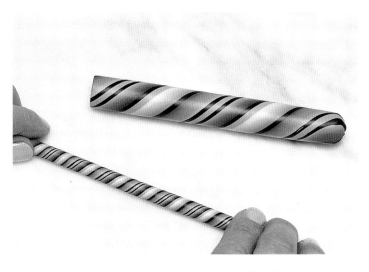

3 Move the clay to the middle of the knitting needle. Pinch the ends to the needle. Roll and twist the clay on the needle. When the diameter of the tube is small, the easiest way to twist is to hold one end of the needle stationary and either push the opposite end away from you or pull it toward you—not both. Use whichever movement you're more comfortable with.

4 Loosen the clay by firmly holding the skewer while twisting the clay. Press a side of the Marxit (I'm using the 15mm side) against the loosened clay. Either remove the clay from the needle and lay it straight on a sheet of polyester batting or bake the clay on the needle. Bake for 15 minutes at 300°F.

5 When the clay is cool, you may cut the beads, following the impressed lines. For the eyeglass leash, you'll need approximately thirty 15mm beads. For the stringing: Alternate small glass beads with polymer beads until your leash is the desired length. I string my beads on heavy fishing line and haven't had breakage trouble yet. You may use eyeglass leash findings or small O rings. To finish each end, string fourteen seed beads on the fishing line. Thread through the O ring. Thread the end of the line back through the second bead you strung. With a cigarette lighter, melt the end of the fishing line to form a plastic "bead." Pull the line through. Secure the other end in the same way.

Squiggly Beads

**FOR ONE BEAD,
YOU WILL NEED:**

Clay

Pasta machine

Knitting needle or
brass tube for
smoothing

Nublade

Needle tool

Scalpel or X-Acto-type
craft knife

EVERYONE LOVES these bright, colorful beads. (I call them squiggly beads, but some people call them cucumbers.) Use them for bracelets, necklaces, and more. They are very striking, yet easy to make, and you can vary the colors, the shapes, and the squiggles to your creative heart's content.

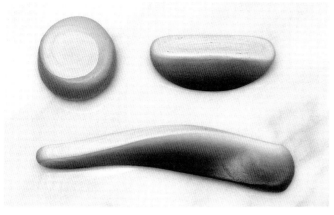

1 (TOP LEFT) Start by making a Skinner Blend striped cane. First, make a Skinner Blend sheet and roll it into a plug. (TOP RIGHT) Pinch the top of the plug as shown. Then flip it over and pinch the bottom. By keeping the plug on your work surface as you work, you will begin to stretch the Skinner Blend sideways. (BOTTOM) Continue pinching and stretching the piece out to form a strip approximately twice the thickness of the thickest setting of the pasta machine. Note: Try not to make this strip too tall—no more than 1 inch tall. It should look like a long, thin Skinner Blend strip that is twice the thickness of the thickest setting on the pasta machine.

2 Roll a sheet of a contrasting color through a medium-thin setting of the pasta machine. Place the strip on the sheet as shown on the left, leaving a margin on both sides and at one end. (The reason they are not the same size will be apparent.) Roll the piece through the thickest setting of the pasta machine. Note: The last thing that should roll through the machine is the extra clay at one end of the contrasting color sheet. The rolled sheet might look something like the one on the right. If it does, cut the excess clay from the sides and straighten out the strip. (As you rolled the strip and sheet through the machine, the thicker strip spread out. A sheet trimmed to exactly the same dimensions as the strip would have left the edges of the strip uncovered by the sheet.)

3 (TOP) Cut the strip in half and stack one half atop the other. As you can see, the stripes are thick. (CENTER) Roll the double-thick strip through the machine again. Here, the stripes are thinner. The red stripes separating the Skinner Blend are still very apparent. (BOTTOM) Cut the strip in half and stack one half atop the other. Repeat to make a thick slab. Trim the sides with a blade. Here is the finished cane.

4 (LEFT) For the squiggly beads: Cut thin pieces from a Skinner Blend striped cane. Place the slices around your bead core (here you can see the scrap clay wrapped with white). Place slices around to cover the core. (RIGHT) Cover the ends of the scrap clay exposed at the ends of the cylinder. To do this, grasp the cylinder with your thumb and first finger and gently depress the ends. Working one end at a time, smooth the clay from the sides over the scrap ends, rotating as you go until the scrap has been covered. If any of the core is still showing, press it in with a pointed but blunt tool, such as a large-gauge knitting needle or crochet hook, and then smooth the clay over to cover.

5 (LEFT) Form the clay into an elongated almond shape by pinching and gently pulling the clay at the ends. Refine the points by rolling the clay gently against your work surface. If the stripes twist, untwist them to straighten the lines with your fingers. (CENTER) Now it's time to make the squiggle. Begin at one end and push the point around and down to make a pleasing curve. (RIGHT) Finish shaping the bead by gently pushing the opposite end up and around to make an even spiral. Drill the hole with a needle tool.

6 These beads are not evenly weighted, so you must consider how you would like the bead to hang. Here are some additional shapes you might try. When making a shape such as the squiggle on the far left, begin by shaping the curl at the top. To make the additional curves, I put my finger on the right side of the bead and bent the clay around my finger. I then moved my finger to the left side of the bead and bent the clay around. Finally I return to the right side and bent the clay around my finger, finishing the curves. Nest the beads in baking soda and cure for 30 minutes at 300°F.

SKINNER BLEND BULLSEYE CANE

YOU'VE LEARNED how to make Skinner Blends and how to make Skinner Blend plugs, and you've tried your hand at squiggly beads. Now let's look at some ways to use your Skinner Blends in millefiori work, starting with a versatile Skinner Blend bullseye cane.

1 Make a Skinner Blend. At this point, if you've made your Skinner Blend using the thickest setting of the pasta machine, you could continue, but the bullseye cane would have a recognizable swirl pattern. If this is the effect you want, continue with the instructions. For a finer, almost imperceptible shading, reset the pasta machine to thinner settings and roll the blend through again and again until it reaches the desired thinness, always placing a solid-color edge on the rollers.

2 Decide which color you'd like to see in the center of the cane. Trim that edge. To avoid the appearance of a large solid-color center, cut that edge close to the point where you see the colors beginning to change. You want some of your original color, so don't cut it all off! From the cut edge, roll up tightly to the opposite edge. If the color at the opposite edge doesn't roll once around the entire cane, trim that edge, roll clay of the same color through the pasta machine at the same thickness as the sheet, and wrap this new sheet once around.

3 Trim the ends. This simple cane may be used as it is, but it also forms the basis for many other cane patterns.

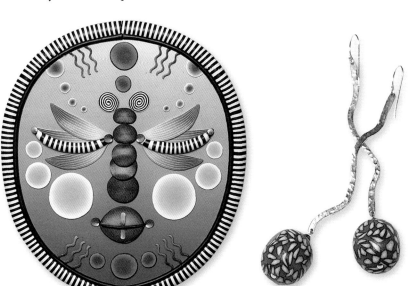

FAR LEFT: DONNA KATO
This mask uses elements of Skinner Blend bullseye canes.

LEFT: NATALIA GARCIA
The beads on these earrings were made with a freeform Skiner Blend bullseye cane. Natalia also did the silver work.

BASIC MONARCH BUTTERFLY CANE

MY FRIEND, artist Connie Donaldson, has a special affinity for butterflies, and her beautiful work is a testament to that fact. Her way of making her canes, featured in *Polymer Café* magazine, differs from mine. Here's a look at how I make mine.

1 From red and orange clay, make a Skinner Blend. Divide it in half. Roll each half down through a medium thin setting of the pasta machine. For the bullseye canes: Roll one piece from red to orange. Roll the other piece from orange to red. Wrap both bullseye canes with a thin sheet of black clay.

2 Roll a cylinder of white clay. Wrap the cylinder with two sheets of black clay that have been rolled through the thickest setting of the pasta machine. Cut this wrapped cylinder in half, dividing it into two pieces of equal length.

DONNA KATO
ABOVE: *Butterfly canes flutter across these three beads.*
RIGHT: *These shoes, made for our Feat of Clay show, feature a large butterfly cane.*

Wrap one half cylinder with an additional sheet of black clay, also rolled through the thickest setting of the pasta machine. When they are reduced and used, you will have dots in two sizes.

3 The monarch butterfly wing begins as you shape the top of the wing; this part is larger than the others that you will add. I reduce the canes as I need to, reducing one end of a cane and leaving the opposite end large. Reduce and cut 2 inches off one end of one of the Skinner Blend bullseye canes. As shown, reshape the round section into an elongated teardrop shape.

4 Reduce a 2-inch section from the other Skinner Blend bullseye cane. This piece should be smaller in diameter than the first. Reshape this piece into an elongated teardrop shape and press it below the first, aligning the points of the teardrops together.

5 Further reduce a 2-inch section of one of the canes, making the reduction smaller than the last one. Reshape the section and press it below the second as shown.

6 Repeat two more times to make a wing with five sections; decreasing in size as shown.

7 Reduce the two white-and-black Skinner Blend bullseye canes. Place them randomly along the side of the wing.

8 With your fingers, compress the pieces to the wing. Finish by rolling with a rod. Your wing is finished. While this simplified wing is not anatomically correct, I use it for both the top and bottom wings on my butterflies. When I make butterflies, I place the bottom wings on first, roll them into the base clay, then add the top wings.

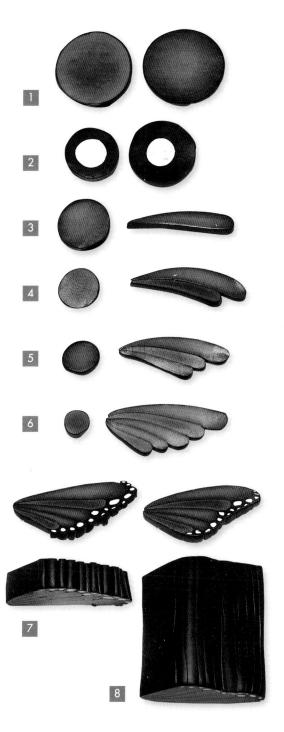

SKINNER BLEND IKAT CANE

DONNA KATO
All four of these pieces were made using Skinner Blend ikat canes.

EARLIER IN THIS BOOK, I showed ways of making ikat canes that began with a checkerboard. This method, which begins with a Skinner Blend setup, also results in the ikat pattern for results that are not identical to that earlier cane, but similar in appearance.

1 Begin with a basic two-part Skinner Blend setup as shown on page 109.

2 Onto this sheet, randomly place strips of white clay (you may use other colors, too).

3 Position this sheet on the rollers of the pasta machine as if you were making a Skinner Blend, then roll through.

4 From one two-color edge, roll toward the opposite edge. This piece has been turned—make sure you roll from an edge with two colors.

5 Compress this cylinder to form a plug. The plug should be only one color on the bottom and the other color on top.

6 Flatten the plug into a strip approximately ¼-inch thick with your fingers, then roll over the strip with an acrylic rod to smooth. It is best to make the strip thinner than your finished cane. Placing a short side on the rollers, roll through.

7 Fold the long strip in half and place one half atop the other. As you can see, the pattern is rather coarse, so roll the strip through again, starting with a short edge on the rollers.

8 Cut in half and stack one half atop the other. The pattern is finer, but still on the coarse side, so roll the stack through and then stack again. For my cane, I rolled through and stacked one last time. If you roll through too many times, you'll end up losing the ikat effect, so check after each time you roll through before dividing and rolling through again.

9 When you like the effect, cut the strip in half and place one half atop the other, offsetting the pieces. (Alternatively, rather than offsetting the pieces, you might try stacking them so the stripes line up or even flipping them over so the colors are in opposition.)

10 Now cut this cane in half and stack the pieces in whichever way you choose. Make sure you like the effect.

11 Trim the sides of the cane to make a neat slab. Here is my finished Skinner Blend ikat cane.

SKINNER BLEND IKAT
SNAIL-TYPE JELLYROLL CANE

THIS IKAT CANE does not include the random white pieces of the Skinner Blend cane that we just explored. You may add them if you like the additional texture in the cane. This cane is made with deep crimson (one part ultra blue to fifteen parts red) and pale yellow (a pinch of yellow added to white).

1 Begin with a basic two-color Skinner Blend setup. Trim the four sides with a blade. Then, as if you were making a complete Skinner Blend, roll the sheet through the thickest setting of the pasta machine. Fold the sheet, same color edge on same color edge, place the fold on the rollers, and roll through. Repeat four more times. Cut the sheet in half, perpendicular to the solid-color edges. Place one half atop the other.

2 Cut the sheet in half again and stack. You now have four layers.

3 Trim the solid-color edges that probably have become ragged as you rolled the clay through. With the acrylic rod, thin and taper the two solid-color edges. Then roll a thin sheet of your stripe color. Place the partially blended stack on the thin sheet and trim the excess clay around.

4 From one tapered edge, roll up tightly. Here is the finished cane.

This picture shows some of the infinite possibilities for ikat jellyroll canes. Note the rainbow canes, made with three-part Skinner Blends.

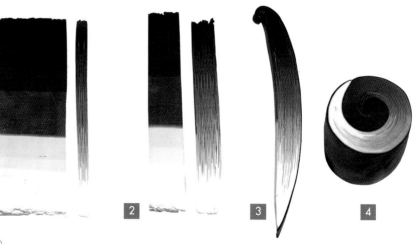

1 2 3 4

DONNA KATO

Elements of this pendant were made with Skinner Blend ikat slabs and jellyrolls. The cord is glued into the top piece at the right. It slides through the top piece at the left, the round bead, and the piece with the square hole. It is glued into the bottom piece.

TRANSLUCENT CANES

I began making Tanslucent Overlay Beads when I worked for Eberhard Faber in 1998. As part of their Fimo Soft line, they offered several translucent colors. I had experimented with using translucent clay to make imitation opals and the like, and my tests became a game with me—how many layers could I overlap and still see through to the first? Later I developed translucent Skinner Blend canes, incorporating translucent Skinner Blends separated by a simple white stripe.

DONNA KATO
A mix of translucent canes and opaque canes were used to make these two sophisticated pendants.

SIGAL BEN-HAIM
Sigal's beautiful hamsa was made with translucent and opaque Skinner Blend canes, floral canes, and stamping, then sealed with a two-part cold enamel finish.

TRANSLUCENT SKINNER BLEND STRIPED CANE

Before you create your Translucent Overlay Beads, you will need to create several elements. First, make your translucent Skinner Blend striped cane. Mix two translucent colors by mixing a small amount of colored clay into translucent clay. If the color is too pale, mix more color into the clay. Following the instructions for the Skinner Blend striped cane (see page 117), construct the cane. As the colors are translucent, I usually use light, opaque colors for the stripes. If you wish to use a dark-colored stripe in this cane, it is best to sandwich the color between thin sheets of white that will protect the translucent clay from the influence of the dark stripe.

These translucent Skinner Blend striped canes were used in the beads at left.

DONNA KATO
Translucent striped canes give this bright bracelet an extra dimension of glowing color.

TRANSLUCENT DOT CANE

Next, make your Translucent Dot Cane. These amusing canes feature rings floating in a translucent background. After curing, the translucent clay becomes more clear, making the dots stand out even more.

1 Roll a cylinder of translucent clay. Wrap the cylinder with a thin sheet of white. Then wrap the cylinder with a thin sheet of black. Wrap with another thin sheet of white, making a bullseye cane.

2 Wrap this cane with four or five sheets of translucent clay rolled through the thickest setting of the pasta machine. With a blade, cut four sides to make the cane square.

3 Reduce this square cane to four times its original length. Cut it into four equal pieces, then press two together, side by side, and the other two together side by side. Place one half atop the other. You now have four dots.

4 For smaller rings, reduce the cane again, this time to four times its length. Repeat the division and reassemble to make sixteen rings.

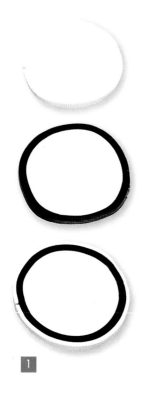

1

2   3   4

FOIL TRANSFERS

For the metallic effect of the Translucent Overlay Beads, master foil transfers. Nancy Banks was the artist who discovered that foil could be used with polymer clay. The following steps show how to transfer foil from mylar to clay.

1 Begin with a thin sheet of clay. I've chosen translucent clay. (I will use this in the Translucent Overlay Beads on page 122.)

2 Place the foil on the clay, mylar side up. You should see the color or pattern of the foil. If you don't, it's upside down. With a bone folder or credit card, burnish the foil to the clay. To burnish, stroke across the surface of the mylar. Stroke in all directions, approximately a hundred times altogether. Be careful not to lift the mylar from the clay.

3 Grasp a corner of the foil and quickly rip the foil from the clay. As you can see, the foil has left the mylar and is now on the clay.

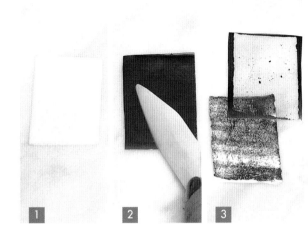

JEANETTE RICHMOND
Jeanette's beads illustrate how foil can be used to create the look of dichroic glass.

JELLYROLL MOKUME GANE

Mokume gane, from the Japanese for "wood-eye metal," is a finish that looks like richly burled wood. In polymer clay, the effects are elegant and exotic. This is mokume gane in cane form. Sharply angled slices spotlight the pattern within the cane.

1 Roll a sheet of translucent clay through the thinnest setting of your pasta machine. Using the foil transfer method, transfer foil to one side of the clay.

2 Foil side up, begin at one edge and roll up tightly. With a sharp blade, cut slices at a steep angle to reveal the foil rings.

RIPPLE-CUT MOKUME GANE

These canes are very similar to the jellyroll mokume gane canes, but using a ripple blade to cut the sharply angled slices adds extra texture and interest.

1 Roll a sheet of translucent clay through the thinnest setting of your pasta machine. Transfer patterned foil onto the clay.

2 Cut the sheet in half and stack one half on top of the other. Continue dividing and stacking until you have a block. With a ripple blade, cut through the block at a steep angle. Make another cut, following the same angle with the ripple blade in registration with the first cut.

DONNA KATO
I used ripple-cut mokume gane to create these two bangle bracelets.

Translucent Overlay Beads

EVERYONE LOVES these beautiful beads, which combine metallic elements with translucent canes to striking visual effect. The success of the beads relies upon the thinness of the slices cut from the canes. The goal is to cut slices so thin that you can see right through the upper slices to the slices below. Although I've given a specific order in which you use the elements, there are no rules. This technique is very forgiving; keep adding and overlaying elements until you are happy. Work a few slices at a time rather than covering the base bead and rolling at the end. The bead made in this project is the one featured at center front in the picture.

1 Roll a base bead of white or another light color, such as pearl. In this photograph, you can see the basic components you will be using in this bead: several translucent Skinner Blend striped canes, a translucent and white jellyroll, a jellyroll mokume gane, a block of ripple-cut mokume gane, and a translucent dot cane.

2 This picture shows how I shave the slices from the canes. Hold the cane at an angle so that, should the blade slip, it will not cut your hand.

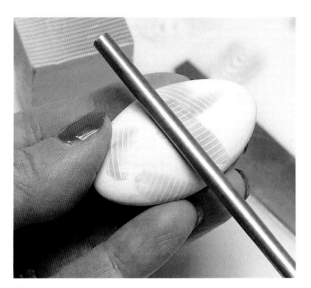

3 Place a few slices on the base bead and roll them in with a brass tube or knitting needle. Roll back and forth in the direction of the stripes. Add a slice cut from the ripple-cut mokume gane block. Roll it in with the rod. Cut slices from the jellyroll mokume gane cane and roll them in with the rod.

4 Finish the bead by cutting from the translucent dot cane and rolling it into the bead, as shown. The surface should be smooth, and you should not be able to feel the edges of the added slices. With a bamboo skewer or needle tool, drill the bead hole. Nest the bead in polyester batting, or in baking soda in a pan, and cure. Sand the bead with a fine-grit sanding block. Wet-sand the bead first with 400-grit, then 600-grit wet/dry sandpaper. Polish by buffing with an electric buffer.

he loves me...
he loves me not?
purple is not
a lifestyle...
lime green is.

FLOWERS, FEATHERS, AND FACES

This section of the book focuses on some more-advanced projects featuring flowers, feathers, and faces. You'll use all the tricks and experience you have gained in the previous sections to make flower jewelry with realistic-looking daisies and Japanese cherry blossoms, floral scenes for display and decoration, an elegant Manju pendant with a feather insert, and, finally, one of my face canes. I've tried to break everything down into simple steps that any of my readers can do with care and patience. Enjoy your new talents!

FLOWER CANES

EVERYONE LOVES flower canes! Flowers, with their neat symmetry and pretty colors, lend themselves to millefiori canes. Creating realistic flower canes is surprisingly easy. Once you have learned the basic techniques, visit a botanical garden or park and study real flowers to get more ideas for your flower canes.

The daisy and the cherry blossom flowers have been "packed" with translucent clay. This increases the possible uses of these canes, as the translucent clay becomes more translucent after curing.

TOP LEFT: DONNA KATO
We trade poker chips at our Clay Carnival events. These were the swapping chips one year!

TOP RIGHT: BRURYA
Caned flowers set in translucent clay grace this hamsa and beads, set in cold enamel.

LEFT: NAAMA ZAMIR
Naama's lovely flower canes were pressed to the back side of a glass bowl.

JEANETTE KANDRAY
*Jeanette turned her flowers
into fishes!*

DAWN NAYLOR
*It's a great idea to save
samples of your canes, like
Dawn does.*

DAISY

The technique used for this daisy, with its eight radiating petals, can be used to create a variety of flowers.

TIP

When a flower has six round petals, the diameter of the center should be equal to the diameter of the petals' diameter. Since these daisy petals are not round, you may need extra petals, or you might need to reduce the diameter of the jellyroll center.

1 Make a Skinner Blend sheet with yellow and white clay. From this sheet, make a bullseye cane.

2 Wrap the bullseye with a thin sheet of black clay. This will help define the edges of the flower petals.

3 Stand the cane up on end and cut down to halve it the long way. Then cut it in half again to make four wedge-shaped pieces. The four wedges will each make two daisy petals.

4 To form the petals: Reshape each wedge by bringing the clay from the perimeter up toward the point of the wedge.

5 The easiest way to do the reshaping is to place a flat side of a wedge against your finger and push the clay toward the point with your thumbs.

6 Press two reshaped wedges together to make a petal. Here you see the side of a cane and a slice cut from it.

7 Beginning at one side of the petal, wrap a medium-thin sheet of translucent clay around to the other side of the petal. Trim. Note: The translucent sheet is not wrapped around the entire petal. With a needle tool, press the translucent sheet into the indented area between the lobes of the petal. Roll a small snake of translucent clay, cut it in half, and press the round side of the snake into the indent. Repeat with the remaining two wedges. You now have two petals.

8 Reduce the two petal canes to 8 inches in length each. Cut each piece into 2-inch lengths to create eight petals. Loosely put the petals together to determine the size of the center. Then make a black-and-white balanced jelly-roll cane (see page 74). Reduce the cane to the size needed for the center of the flower. (Remember, the larger the center, the more petals you need to surround it.) Press the petals to the center. Wrap the entire daisy cane with a medium-thin sheet of translucent clay. With a needle tool, press the translucent sheet into indented areas (between the petals, for example).

9 Roll a snake of translucent clay and fill the indented areas of the cane. With a blade, cut away any excess clay from the translucent snake.

10 Force out the air by compressing the cane. Here is the reduced and finished daisy.

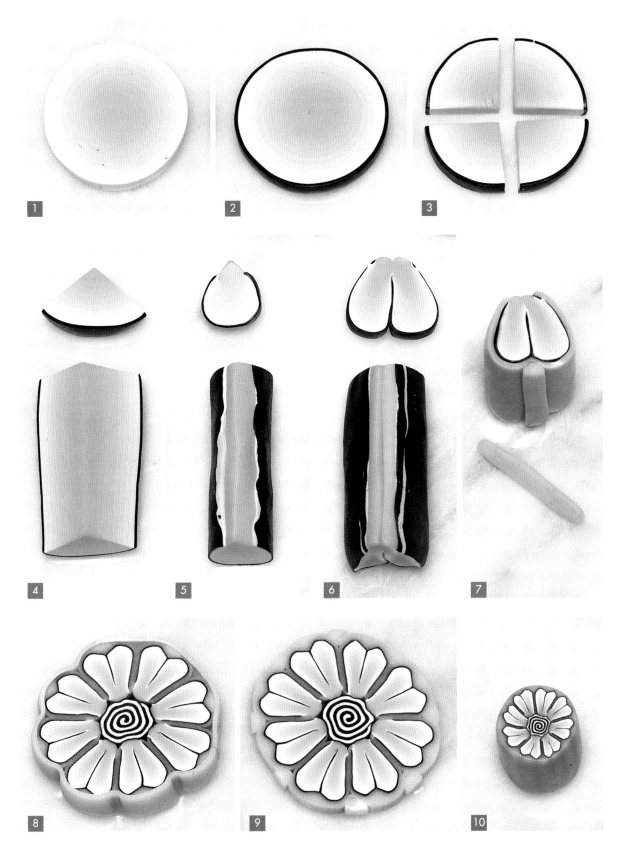

I've used these daisies on a field of faux bone. The translucent packing clay will be less apparent when the piece is cured. As you can see, some of the daisies have flattened and are no longer round—I think they look more realistic and interesting this way.

DONNA KATO
Daisies and leaves, made using the component cane technique, were placed on a painted clay surface to create this hollow bead.

JAPANESE CHERRY BLOSSOM

In Japan, families and friends gather to view cherry blossoms when the trees spring into bloom in the springtime. The blossoms, or sakura, are gone so quickly. But your cherry blossoms will last forever, an eternal reminder of nature's beauty.

1 For the flower center: Roll a cylinder of the center color. Reshape it to a triangle shape.

2 Wrap two sides of the triangle with a thin sheet of white clay.

3 Reduce this piece to a length of 6 inches. Cut it into six pieces of equal length. Press the white sides together so the white lines look like spokes radiating from a point in the center.

4 Roll a cylinder of white clay. At the end of each white "spoke," press a piece of clay.

5 Wrap the cane with a medium-thin sheet of clay the same color as the center.

6 Roll a sheet of clay the same color as the center through the thickest setting of the pasta machine. Cut strips and fill the spaces between the white balls.

7 Squeeze and compress the cane to join the pieces and eliminate air pockets. The white balls will be misshapen, but in the finished cane, that won't matter much.

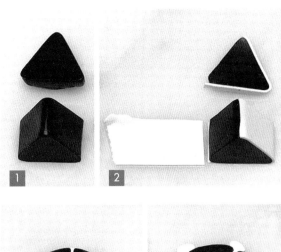

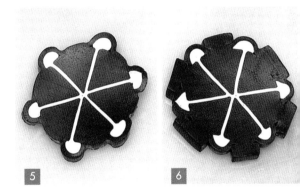

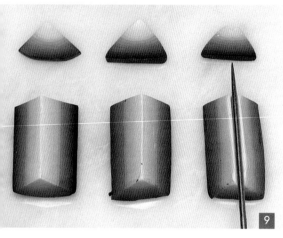

8 Using the same color as the flower center plus white, make a Skinner Blend sheet, then a bullseye cane. Roll the cane tightly from white to the flower center color. You will need five petals to make this flower, so cut the bullseye into two pieces of equal length. Stand each piece up on end and cut it in half, then in half again, to divide each piece into four wedges. There are five petals, so you will have three more wedges than you need.

9 This picture shows how each wedge will be reshaped. On the left, you see the original wedge and, above it, a piece cut from it to show you its shape. Press the round side against your work surface to create a triangle shape. Press the side of a needle tool into the point of the wedge to form an indent in the tip of the petal.

10 Press the five petals against the center to make the complete flower.

11 Wrap the flower with a thin sheet of black. With a needle tool, press the wrapped clay into the indented areas of the flower.

12 Roll a thin snake of translucent clay and place it in the indented area at the tip of each petal to fill the space.

13 Wrap the entire flower with a medium sheet of translucent. This ensures that the black outline will remain smooth.

14 Roll a thick cylinder of translucent clay. Cut the cylinder in half along its length. Press the round side of the half cylinder into the area between each petal.

15 Gently draw the clay over the tips of the flower petals. If necessary, roll a snake of translucent clay and fill any gaps at the petal tips with the snake. Here you can see the snake and how it was used to fill the tips of the petals.

16 To give the cane a perfectly round shape, cut away any excess translucent clay with a blade.

17 Here is the same cane, reduced two different sizes. A variety of sizes, used together, will give a natural effect to a project.

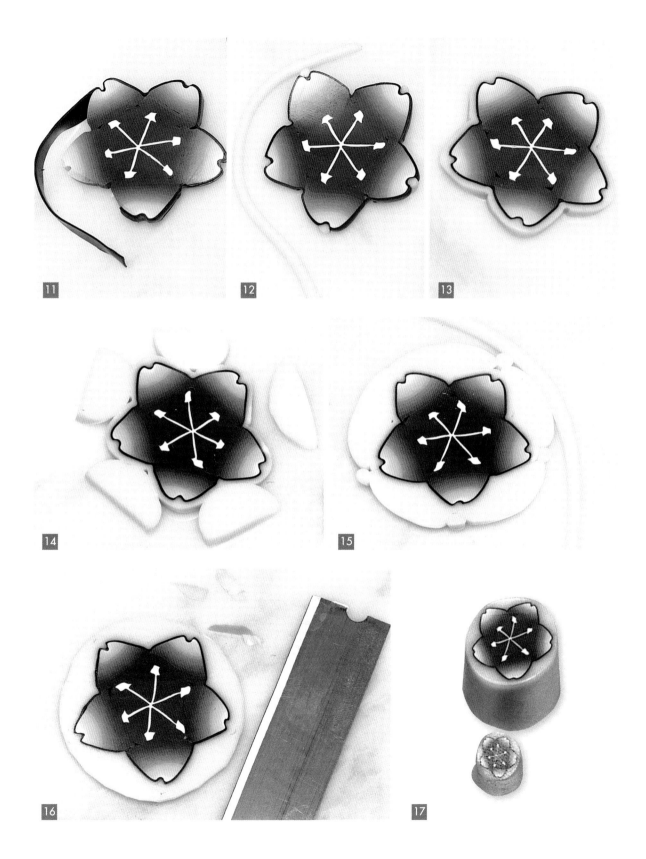

I used the Japanese cherry blossoms in this naturalistic piece.

DONNA KATO

These earrings feature the Japanese cherry blossom cane and leaves on faux bone. I make the basic floral design, then cut it in half to make earrings.

COMPONENT FLOWER CANE

Even my most elaborate floral pieces consist of simple images that are extremely easy to make. You see, the petals of the flowers all come from the same single-petal cane. Even leaves and reeds are made the same way—in different colors, and shaped differently, of course, but the basic steps are the same. Try it yourself!

DONNA KATO
ABOVE: *I used a flask as the base form for this floral purse.*
LEFT: *My egg purse was shaped on a real emu egg.*

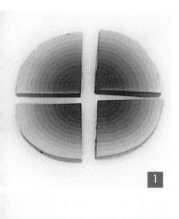

1 Make a Skinner Blend bullseye cane. Trim the ends and stand it upright. Cut down through the standing cane, dividing it in half. Cut it to make four wedges. Don't worry if they're not exactly the same; it won't make any difference.

2 Reshape each piece by gently drawing the clay from the perimeter up toward the point of the wedge. Do this on both sides of each wedge (see the more detailed instructions on the daisy cane, page 138.)

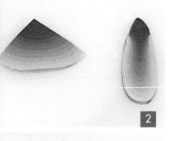

3 Flatten each piece slightly with your fingers and place them side by side, so the points are all on the same side.

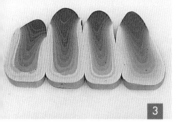

4 Square off this piece, first by flattening the four sides with your fingers, then by rolling each side with a brayer.

5 Cut the cane in half and press the halves together . The effect should be that of teeth in a comb. Force the cane back into a square shape. You will now see eight colored projections.

6 Depending on the degree of contrast between the two colors you have chosen, you may want to stop at this point. For instance, yellow and white do not have much contrast and further reduction, division, and reassembly might make it impossible to see the projections at all. On the other hand, color combinations such as violet and white have a high degree of contrast, and as a result, they maintain clarity through many repeated reductions, divisions, and reassemblies. So, repeat until you are pleased with the appearance of the cane. For my cane, I repeated the process one more time.

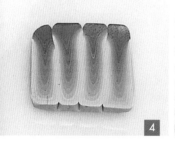

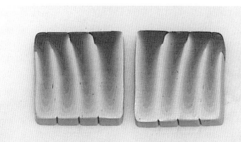

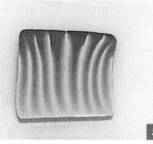

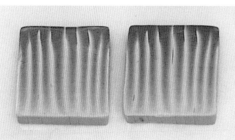

7 Now force the square petal cane into a circular shape by pressing the like-colored corners together. Work along the length of the cane, making sure to pinch the colored corners together, then flip over the cane and pinch the white corners together.

8 The petal shape is achieved by pinching the center of the colored part of the cane. I usually pinch only as much as I need at the time. As you create your floral image, you'll use the largest petals first, then smaller and smaller petals that are made by further reduction.

9 The leaves and reeds are made in leaf-appropriate colors. The leaf shape is made by pinching along one color side, then the opposite color side.

10 The reed is simply an extremely tapered and elongated leaf. Here, you see the original bullseye, the reed on its side, and a piece cut from the reed.

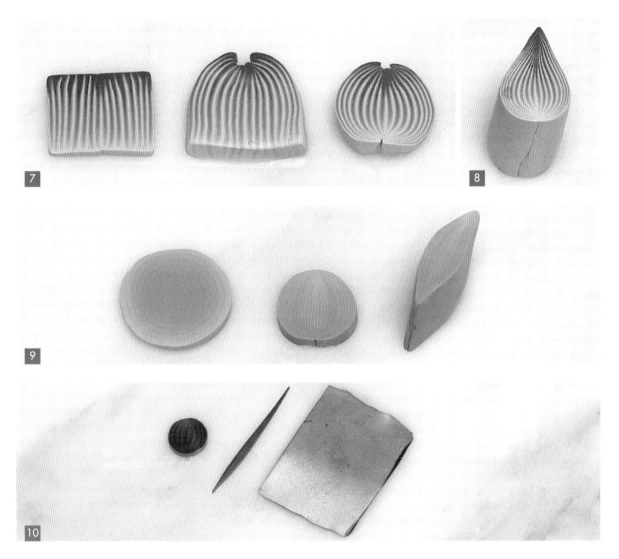

STAR CANE

I use star canes in my floral scenes, where they look pretty against a Skinner Blend evening sky. The shape of the canes makes them "twinkle" like real stars. The technique used to make the star canes is similar to that of making many flower canes.

1 Roll a short cylinder of white clay. Force the cylinder into a triangle shape and reduce it to a length of 5 inches. Cut it into five 1-inch pieces.

2 Roll a small cylinder of white clay approximately the same size as the triangles. Press one edge of one of the triangles to the cylinder. Slide the second triangle beneath the first. Continue sliding the subsequent triangles under until all the triangles are on the cylinder.

3 Roll two cylinders of translucent clay approximately the same diameter and height as the assembled star. Divide each of these two cylinders into four evenly sized wedges, for a total of eight wedges.

4 Press the point of one wedge into the space between two points of the star. Repeat, filling all the spaces between the star points.

5 Push the clay so it fills the space. Note that at this stage, the star looks like a flower.

6 With a blade, cut the excess translucent clay from around the star to make a round cane that can then be reduced.

Floral Scene

FLORAL SCENES may look complicated, and they do take patience and preparation. But every floral scene is made using canes and techniques that you have probably already mastered at this point in the book. Put what you have learned to use, and enjoy the results!

FOR ONE FLORAL SCENE, YOU WILL NEED:

Clay

Pasta machine

Nublade

Ceramic tile

Knitting needle or brass tube

Acrylic rod

Kato Clear Medium

Smoothing tool

Gold acrylic paint

400- and 600-grit wet/dry sandpaper

1 The background here is a basic Skinner Blend of pearl and blue clay. Make your blend. Because you are making a fairly large floral scene, almost any good-sized Skinner Blend sheet will do. (If you were making a pendant or earrings, you would only need a smaller Skinner Blend, which you could cut from a Skinner Blend plug.) Roll the Skinner Blend sheet through a medium setting. Press it onto a ceramic tile, eliminating any air pockets between the tile and the clay. Here are the components and tools I will use in my floral scene. The ceramic tile holds the clay steady and makes it easier to embed slices without stretching and thinning the background clay.

2 The first slices you will apply are the leaves and reeds. Cut the slices as thinly as you can, then start on your scene. Note that these compositions are worked from the bottom up. Do not overlap cane slices. After you have placed a few of the leaves and reeds on the background, roll them flat with a brass rod or a brayer, rolling in all directions so that the slices spread out evenly. Before adding more slices, you should be able to run your fingers across the surface of your floral scene and not feel where the cane slices are.

3 Continue filling in with leaves.

4 Once you are satisfied with your foliage, place the largest row of flower petals. Remember, never overlap slices. Roll these flower petal slices into the clay sheet.

5 Reduce the flower petal cane to make smaller petals, then cut slices and place them on the first row. Roll them into the sheet. You may add other flowers, such as the red petals on the right, at any time.

6 To make the flower stems, cut a slice from your Starry Night zigzag cane and roll it through the pasta machine through thinner and thinner settings, all the way to the thinnest setting. Cut very thin strips from the thinned piece.

7 Reduce the flower petal cane further to make even smaller petals. Cut slices and place them on the second row of petals, then roll them in. I decided that the red flowers weren't what I wanted. As I had not rolled them in, I was able to lift the slices from the scene and replace them with the violet-and-white petals. I've also added the stems, as you can see, and rolled them in.

8 Make a star cane set in translucent clay. Reduce a portion of the star cane, then cut thin slices. Position them in your composition and roll them smooth. Reduce the star cane further, cut, and add more stars to the scene. Reduce the cane further, cut, and add these still smaller stars to the scene. Roll the stars in with an acrylic rod until the surface is completely smooth. Trim the sides of the scene. Bake the clay in the oven for 15 minutes at 275°F. When it is cool, sand with 400-grit, then 600-grit, wet/dry sandpaper.

9 For the frame with raised sides: Roll a medium-thin sheet of black clay. Place the sheet on a ceramic tile. Apply a light coat of Kato Clear Medium to the back of the floral scene, then press it to the sheet of black clay. Next, roll a sheet of black clay through the thickest setting. Fold the sheet in half and roll it with an acrylic rod. Cut four ½-inch strips. Pick up one strip and turn it over—this side will have crisp corners. You can see that the lower strip (which has been turned over) has sharp corners, while the strip above it has corners that appear more rounded. Press one strip to one side of the scene and another strip to the other side of the scene. Holding the blade at an angle, cut the strips only along the bottom of the scene. Remove the excess strip of clay. This clay overhang makes it easier to blend the clay in the next strip to the ones on the sides.

10 Press another strip to the bottom of the scene. As you position the strip at the corners of the scene, push the clay below the overhang. With a sculpture tool, smooth the clay. Finish by smoothing with your fingers. Repeat steps 10 and 11, and add a strip to the top of the piece.

11 To make final cuts, spray your blade with water (this will prevent the clay from sticking to the blade) and cut through all layers of the clay. Cut the sides, the bottom, and the top of the piece.

12 Dab a light coat of gold acrylic paint on the frame. After the first coat is dry, apply another light coat. Apply paint to dry surfaces only; never apply wet paint on wet paint. My piece has four light coats of acrylic paint. Bake the clay at 300°F for 15 minutes. After the piece has cooled, sand the unpainted sides with a fine-grit sanding block. Wipe the sides with a damp cloth. Dab gold acrylic paint onto the sides. Apply the same number of coats to the sides as you did to the front of the frame.

FEATHER CANE

ALTHOUGH THIS FEATHER CANE looks quite complex, it is really very simple to make. The basic feather cane requires two colors for the feather plus a third color to wrap the feather segments. I recommend using white and a color the first time you make this cane. I use gold for my wrap color.

This is a two-color feather cane. Frequently, I make three-color feathers. The difference begins with the basic Skinner Blend setup. If you would like to make a feather featuring three colors, refer to page 110 for instructions on making a three-part Skinner Blend. This simple feather is made of white clay and a blended turquoise (two parts green to three parts turquoise).

ABOVE: DONNA KATO
This pendant features a single feather cane slice, positioned against the sky.

RIGHT: SUSAN WALTER
Susan's beautiful jewelry has both two-dimensional and three-dimensional feathers.

1 Begin with a basic two-color Skinner Blend setup using your chosen feather colors. Roll the Skinner Blend through the pasta machine on the thickest setting. As if you were continuing to make a Skinner Blend, fold the sheet in half and roll it through again. Repeat three more times, for a total of five times folding and rolling the sheet though the pasta machine.

2 Roll the sheet up sideways (*not* from one solid color edge to the other). Cut this cylinder in half, dividing the blend so that one half contains light to medium values and the other piece contains medium to dark.

3 Compress each cylinder by compressing and pushing the ends of each cylinder toward the middle until each is approximately 1 inch tall. Essentially, you have formed two plugs.

4 Place the flattened cylinders on one of their flat sides. Pinch the exposed flat side as shown. Turn each piece over and pinch the other flat side.

5 Roll the flattened pieces lightly. The cut pieces show what they look like inside.

6 Roll gold clay through a very thin setting of the pasta machine. Wrap the thin sheet around each element, leaving a space that will serve as a registration strip.

7 Reduce each piece to a diameter of ¼ inch. With your fingers, pinch along both sides of the registration strip.

8 Roll each piece through the pasta machine down to a medium-thin setting (I use setting 4 on my Makin's machine). The pinching will keep the piece from twisting and rolling through the wrong way. These pieces will be used to make the feather cane.

9 Assemble your feather. The top piece shows what the cane looks like sitting flat on your work surface. The bottom row shows what the cane might look like from your perspective as you put it together. Begin by stacking five pieces straight up.

10 With your fingers, push one side down to make a triangle-shaped cane. By flattening one side, you now have a good angle on which to apply the rest of the feather segments.

11 As you add segments, change from one of your two colored pieces to the other. You may even flip these pieces over so that sometimes the light end of a piece is out and sometimes the dark end is out.

12 For the quill: Roll a cylinder of white. Wrap it with a thin sheet of gold. Flatten the cylinder and taper one side to make a long, tapering teardrop shape.

13 Pick up the feather cane and turn it over. With a rod, flatten and smooth this side of the feather. (This is the inside of the feather, not the outside.)

14 Cut the feather in half. Place the quill against one half of the feather as shown. Make sure you align the tapered edge with the flattened point from step 10. (Note: Quills do not extend to the very tips of feathers.)

15 Press the other piece against the quill as shown. This is a complete feather, with all of the elements in place.

16 This feather is rather oddly shaped! To make it a more conventional shape, pinch the tip of the feather.

17 Here is the finished feather cane along with several other feather canes I have made.

9

10

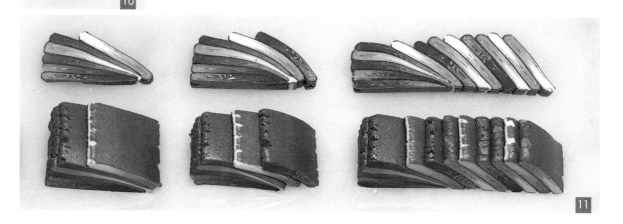

11

Convex Manju Pendant with Feather

**FOR ONE
PENDANT, YOU
WILL NEED:**

Clay

Pasta machine

Kato Clear Medium

Acrylic rod

Scalpel or X-Acto-type
craft knife

Metal foil (I used gold)

Cutting blade

Metal sculpture tool
for blending clay

Coarse sandpaper
or sanding block

Fine metal file for
sanding

2½-inch-diameter
round cutter

Christmas tree ball
or burned-out
lightbulb

Ceramic tile

Hand drill

Buna cord for hanging

Cyanoacrylate glue
such as Kato
Polyglue

THIS ELEGANT LARGE PENDANT makes a striking statement whenever you wear it. The central panel can showcase any insert you like; I've chosen a feather motif here, which gives the pendant a Southwestern feel. Try flowers or an abstract pattern to get different effects. You might even make a small floral panel to fit into the frame.

1 For the focal piece and frame: Roll a sheet of black clay through a medium-thin setting of the pasta machine. Cut a 2-inch square. Onto the square, apply gold foil to the clay. Cut a slice from the feather cane and press it to the foiled clay. (The feather should not be too large; ideally you should be able to cut a 1-inch square with the feather placed diagonally.) Cut a 1-inch square around the feather cane. Place the square with the feather cane on a piece of scrap clay rolled through a medium thin setting of the pasta machine. Roll a sheet of black clay through the thickest setting of the pasta machine. Cut it in thirds and stack the pieces one atop the other to make a thick slab. Then cut four ½-inch-wide strips. In log cabin quilt fashion, place the four strips around the feather piece. Lightly smooth the seams with a sculpture tool and your fingers.

2 Using a blade, cut the four sides, leaving thin walls. It is helpful to spray the blade with water before cutting. Bake this piece for 20 minutes at 300°F. Allow the piece to cool, then lightly sand the sides and the top edge with coarse sandpaper or a sandpaper block.

3 For the pendant: Roll a sheet of clay through a medium-thin setting of the pasta machine. Place the cured focal piece, with its frame, on the black clay. Center a cutter 2½ inches in diameter over the piece.

4 Cut the clay with the cutter. With a scalpel, cut around the focal piece and remove the cutout.

5 Press the circle with the square cutout onto a Christmas tree ornament or a burned-out lightbulb. Work carefully and don't press too hard—the glass is thin! I find it easiest to press the clay at the sides of the cut-out square to the bulb first, then ease up and press the clay at the corners. Bake this piece at 300°F for 20 minutes. When the clay is cured and cool, remove it from the glass. With a coarse-grit sanding block, sand the edges. Place the focal piece on your work surface. Over it, place the convex piece. If the opening is too small and will not slide over the focal piece, sand it to make it fit. Keep sanding and comparing until the convex piece fits over the focal piece. Put the focal piece in the convex frame.

6 For the hanger: Your pendant will need a place for you to glue the cord later. Determine which way your pendant will hang and make a quick sketch showing how it will hang. Turn the piece over. Roll two club-shaped pieces of clay. Fit one piece around one corner and the other around the other corner, from which the pendant will hang.

7 For the backing: Roll a medium-thin sheet of black clay and place it on a ceramic tile. Smear a little Kato Clear Medium onto the back of the focal piece and the edge of the convex frame. Press them to the black sheet. With a scalpel, cut around the pendant. Bake this in the oven for another 15 minutes at 300°F.

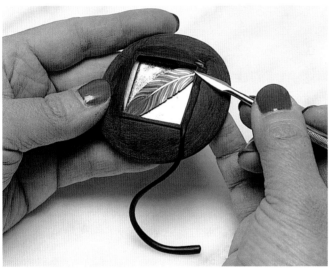

8 If the corners of the focal piece are poking up above the convex piece, they must be sanded down with a coarse-grit sanding block. Then fill the space between the focal piece and the convex piece by rolling a thin snake of black clay. Press the clay snake into the space and smooth with a sculpture tool, then your fingers. Apply a light coat of Kato Clear Medium to the front of the pendant.

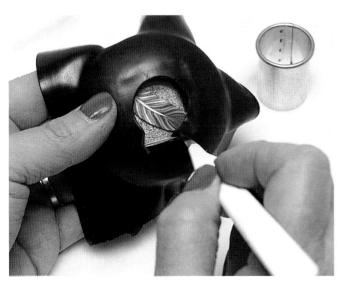

9 Roll a thin sheet of black clay. With a small cutter (I used a circle cutter, but the shape isn't important), cut a piece from the sheet. The cutout makes it easier to cut the clay out over the focal piece. Center the cutout over the focal piece. Press the clay to the front of the pendant. With a scalpel, cut and remove the clay over the focal piece, as shown. With a scalpel or blade, trim the clay from the bottom of the pendant. With your fingers, smooth the raw clay to the back of the piece. Bake for 15 minutes at 300°F. With a fine-grit sanding block, sand the piece front and back.

10 With a hand drill, drill hanging holes. Bake again for 5 minutes at 300°F to matte the finish and heal the sanding marks. Glue the cord into the holes with cyanoacrylate glue.

11 For the closure: (TOP AND CENTER LEFT) Roll a sheet of black clay through the thickest setting of the pasta machine. Cut two pieces approximately 1½ × 1 inches. Then cut a strip approximately ½ inch wide and another strip ¼ inch wide. Center the ½-inch-wide piece on one of the 1½-×-1-inch pieces. Place the ¼-inch strip to the left of the center strip, leaving a space of approximately ⅛ inch. Leaving a space of ⅛ inch, place another ¼-inch strip to the right of the center strip. (BOTTOM LEFT) Place the second 1½-×-1-inch piece on the assembled piece. (RIGHT) With a blade, cut the desired shape. Use oven-safe tools or toothpicks to hold the slots open as you work and during curing.

12 For the cord holders: Roll an almond-shaped bead in black clay. Cut it in half. Restore the shape of each cone with your fingers. Bake all three pieces for 20 minutes at 300°F. Sand all pieces with a fine-grit sanding block. Return to the oven for 5 minutes. Drill holes in the flat end of each cone. Glue each cord end into a cone.

ONE OF THE MOST challenging canes to make is the face cane. Different artists have different methods—some start with a drawing, which is a very good idea for beginners. A simple drawing will provide a template for you to follow and will help you understand the shapes you need to make certain features, as well as the spacing between the features themselves. If you do use a drawing, bear in mind that the eyes will be made one time, then reduced and divided in two, so you'll have to compensate for that and make the clay eye larger than the one you have drawn.

I don't generally begin with a drawing. I start with the eyes, then I do the nose, then the mouth. These features are made independently, overpacked, and then cut square or rectangular. As I work, I reduce the various features to create the final face. My method may not be the most efficient, as I usually find myself with leftover eye and lip canes! These features eventually find their way into another cane. If you mix your face color, make sure you have mixed enough to finish the face, or take notes so you can reproduce the color by following your mixing recipe.

I have used Kato Polyclay Beige straight out of the package. Bearing in mind that I do often have leftover eye and lip canes, this time I used five 3-ounce packages of clay. Kato Polyclay Beige is translucent, not opaque, which adds a lifelike effect to the face. This face is also an example of how placing a dark color next to a translucent color can help create the look of shading in an image.

DONNA KATO
This piece is from my cartoon series.

KIM KORRINGA
Three faces peer out from Kim's enchanting pin.

RHONDA COLCORD
Rhonda's animal-face canes are simple and surprising.

1 For the pupil and iris: To make the pupil, roll a snake of black clay (mine was approximately ⅛ inch in diameter and 2 inches in length). To make the iris, roll a sheet of white clay through a thick setting of the pasta machine and a sheet of the chosen eye color through the same setting. Cut a thin strip from the white sheet and lay it on the black snake. Butt the eye-color sheet against the white strip and wrap around. Trim neatly to make a butt join. Roll to smooth and join the seams.

2 Repeat the process using both the white and the eye-color clay. Roll to smooth.

3 Wrap the cylinder with a thin sheet of the eye color and a thinner sheet of black clay.

4 Make a triangle-shaped piece of white clay. Make sure it is long enough to lay against both sides of the iris. With a knitting needle or other round tool, indent one side of each triangle, forming an even convex shape.

5 Cut the indented white piece in half and press the white pieces against the iris as shown.

6 Stand the cane up on end. Most of the time, our entire iris is not exposed, so trim away the top of the iris with the blade. For my cartoon series, I want a wide-open, surprised eye, so I trim only a bit from the top of the eye. For a sleepy eye, I would cut away more—that is, I would cut farther down toward the pupil.

7 Trim the bottom of the iris and cut away until you are satisfied with the overall shape of the eye.

8 With a knitting needle or other smoothing tool, roll around the eye to smooth its surface.

9 To add shading to the eye: Mix some of the eye color with black clay. Mix white with black to form gray. Roll each of the two mixtures through a thick setting of the pasta machine. Cut a strip of the dark eye color clay the same width as the iris. Press it to the side of the cane as shown.

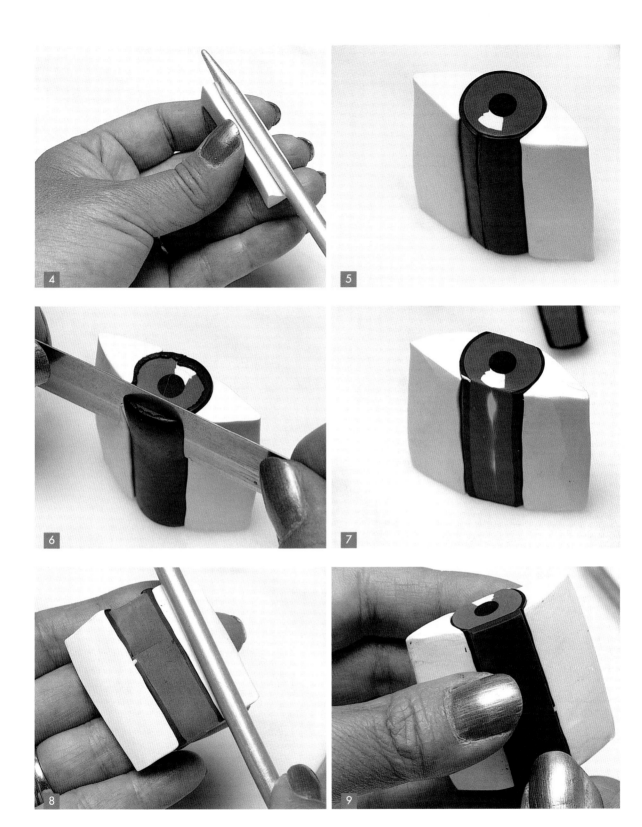

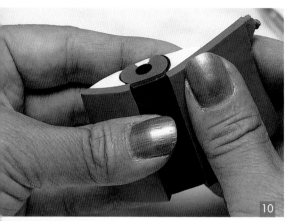

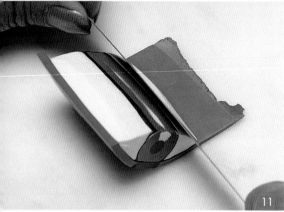

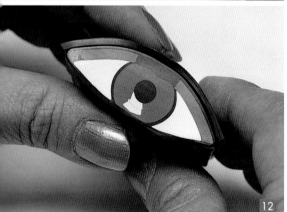

10 To define the eye, place the gray clay next to the dark eye color as shown.

11 Trim the excess gray clay away by laying the blade on the white clay and cutting down to make an angled cut.

12 Wrap the entire eye with a thin sheet of black clay. Roll a piece of black clay through a thick setting of the pasta machine. Gently lay the piece across the top of the eye and trim so it is the exact size, as shown in this picture. Peel this clay off the top of the eye.

13 Taper both ends of the black clay by rolling it with a knitting needle or other smoothing tool.

14 Lay the black piece back on top of the eye. It should be long enough to curl a bit at the end at the outside of the eye to create the appearance of eyelashes.

15 Mix the eye shadow color. Roll a sheet through the thickest setting and stack one piece on the other. Taper one end of the sheet. Place the tapered edge at the outside of the eye and press the sheet across the top of the eye. With a blade, trim away the excess.

16 For the shadow at the inner eye, mix the flesh-tone clay with a bit of brown. Roll through a thick setting of the pasta machine and make a slab composed of four sheets. Taper one end. Line up the tapered edge with the middle of the eye and press it to the inner corner of the eye. With a blade, cut away the excess.

17 Roll a thick sheet of flesh-tone clay. Lay it across the top of the eye. Make a thick slab of flesh color. Round one end. Press it across the top of the eye as shown.

18 With a needle tool, draw where the eyebrow will be placed. With a blade, cut away the excess.

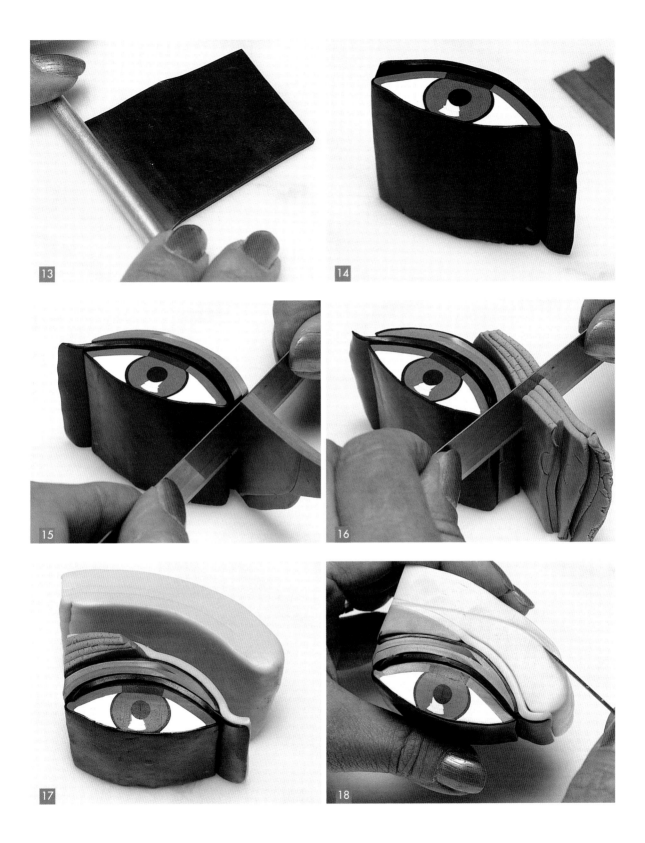

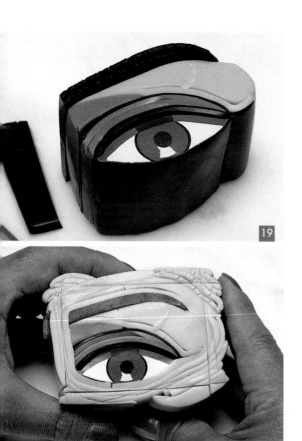

19 Roll a medium-thick sheet of black. Cut it in half and place one half on top of the other. Taper one end of the sheet. Place the tapered edge above the outer edge of the eye. Press the clay to the top of the eye. Trim away the excess.

20 Pack flesh-colored clay around the eye. Draw a rectangle on one end of the cane. With a blade, trim away the excess clay.

21 Reduce the eye cane to half its original size. Cut it in half. Make a block of flesh-colored clay. Place the block between the two eyes. If they are too close, add another sheet (or more) until the spacing looks correct. Trim away the clay from the block neatly so you have a tidy rectangle as shown. Note: Depending on the size of your eye, you may wish to reduce it further. When you look at the eye, try to visualize just how big the final face will be. (Leftover eyes can be used to make another cane, but you don't want to run out of your flesh-colored clay!) For the nostrils: Form a tapering piece of black clay as shown. Wrap it twice with flesh-colored clay. Reduce the nostril until it is twice its original length. Cut it in half.

22 Roll a cylinder of flesh-colored clay. Cut it in half, then in half again to make four wedges. Press one nostril on one side of a wedge and another nostril on the other.

23 Place two more wedges against the nostrils. Cut the remaining wedge in half and press it into the space, as shown. Pack flesh-colored clay around and cut the cane into a square.

24 For the lips: Here you can see the nostrils and the beginning of the mouth. To make the mouth, mix your lip color. Roll the clay into a cylinder and wrap it with a very thin sheet of black. Stand the cane up on end and cut through, dividing it in half. Cover the flat side of one piece with a thin sheet of black. This is the upper lip.

25 Relaxed upper lips don't usually have a straight line along the top; there's a dip down in the center of the upper lip. To make the dip, press the length of the cane on both sides of the center.

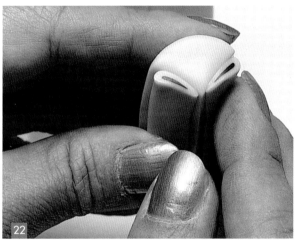

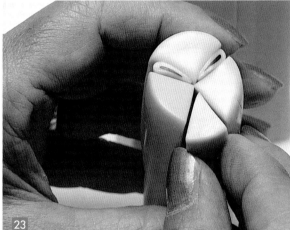

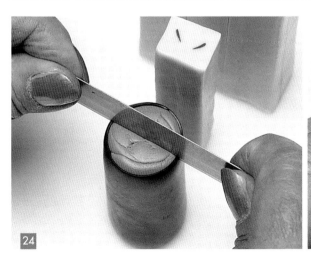

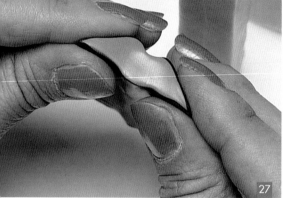

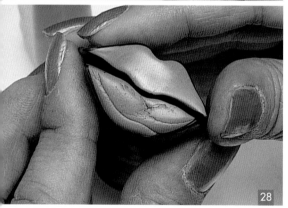

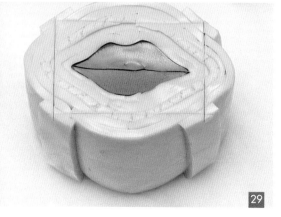

26 Then, to make the indent in the top of the upper lip, press along the length of the middle of the cane as shown. When you are done, the upper lip cane should look like an upside-down W.

27 With your fingers, pinch to refine the corners of the lips, bringing them out along both sides to form a more almond shape.

28 For the lower lip: Indent the center of the inside of the lower lip by pressing along its length. This indent will fit the dip in the upper lip. Pinch along both sides of the lower lip to bring the corners out to the same or nearly the same width as the upper lip. Press the two halves of the lips together.

29 Wrap the lips with a sheet of flesh-colored clay, then pack flesh clay around, as shown. Draw a rectangle around the lips and trim away the excess clay.

30 Reduce the lips until you are satisfied with the size. Press the nostrils to the lips. If there is not enough space between them, place a sheet or sheets of clay between the two features. Here you can see the basic arrangement and spacing of the features. Now all you have to do is fill the square or rectangular spaces with clay.

31 Here is the packed face. As you can see, I've used thick slabs, composed of many sheets to pack the area around the features.

32 Here is the reduced face. I keep the face cane as a square or rectangle while I reduce it.

33 After the face cane has been reduced, I add more clay to make the cane face-shaped.

NOTE

In the cane's rectangular shape, I realized that the nostrils and the lips were too close together. When I packed to make the face oval, I cut the cane straight across between the nostrils and lips and added a sheet of clay to increase the distance between them. I then pressed the clay together so there were no spaces. So you can correct the spacing of features even after the cane is reduced.

30

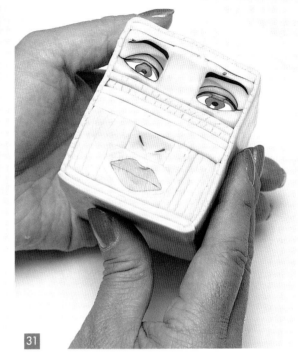

31

32

33

MIRROR IMAGING

INEVITABLY, YOU WILL HAVE WASTE at the ends of your face canes. Here's an interesting way to use these scraps to create realistic or fantasy animal heads. Adding other canes, and even crystals, enhances these otherworldly fellows.

1 From your face cane end, cut a ½-inch piece. You need rather thick slices to stretch and form a shape.

2 Cut this piece in half to make two ¼-inch slices. Open the cut and press the matching sides together, thus forming a mirror image.

3 To elongate the face, gently stretch the clay. In some cases, you will want to add scrap clay for support.

4 If you want to create eye sockets, press the clay in with your thumbs. As you shape, the important thing to remember is never to slide your fingers across the surface. That would smear the canes.

5 To create horns, cut through the slices and gently bend them upward, or twist and roll two snakes together.

6 Additional cane slices may be added to create eyelids, noses, and so on. Each face will be different.

SHANE SMITH
Shane's masterful three-dimensional animal heads are stunningly surreal.

DONNA KATO

These mirror-image animals began as leftover face canes. Some were made from cane ends made by Jana Roberts Benzon.

SUPPLIERS

Listed here are the manufacturers and suppliers of the materials used in this book. Most of these companies sell their products to retail and online stores, which are the most reliable sources for polymer clay supplies. Contact the companies directly to find a retailer near you.

Visit Donna Kato on the Web at www.donnakato.com, and watch her online polymer clay show www.thepolymerclayshow.com, where you can get great tips and ideas for using Kato Polyclay.

AMACO
6060 Guion Road
Indianapolis, IN 46254-1222
(800) 374-1600
www.amaco.com
Polymer clay tools, Poly Tools

FIRE MOUNTAIN GEMS
1 Fire Mountain Way
Grants Pass, OR 97526-2373
1-800-423-2319
www.firemountaingems.com
Kato Polyclay, beads, findings

KEMPER ENTERPRISES
13595 12th Street
Chino, CA 91710
(909) 627-6191
www.kempertools.com
Clay-related tools

MAKIN'S USA INC.
12305 Cary Circle, #4
Omaha, NE 68128
Tel: (402) 891-0085
www.makinsclay.com
Polymer clay, tools

POLYFORM PRODUCTS CO.
1901 Estes Avenue
Elk Grove Village, IL 60007
www.sculpey.com
Sculpey products

POLYMER CLAY EXPRESS
9890 Main Street
Damascus, MD 20872
Phone: (301) 482-0399
www.polymerclayexpress.com
Polymer clays, tools

PRAIRIE CRAFT CO.
P.O. Box 209
Florissant, CO 80816-0209
(888) 603-8332
www.prairiecraft.com
Kato Polyclay, Kato tools and videos, Foredom buffer, books, Makin's Clay pasta machine, and tools

STAEDTLER, INC.
21900 Plummer Street
Chatsworth, California 91311
(800) 776-5544
www.staedtler.us
Fimo products

VALKAT DESIGNS
P.O. Box 12563
Columbus, OH 43212
(614) 279-4790
www.valkatdesigns.com
Precise-A-Slice cane slicer

VAN AKEN INTERNATIONAL
9157 Rochester Court
P.O. Box 1680
Rancho Cucamonga, CA 91729
(909) 980-2001
www.katopolyclay.com
Kato Polyclay, Kato Clear Medium, Jazz Tempera Paint

CONTRIBUTING ARTISTS

CRISTINA ALMEIDA
Lisbon, Portugal

MEISHA BARBEE
San Diego, California

RICHARD BASSETT
Bartow, Florida

JUDY BELCHER
St. Albans, West Virginia

SIGAL BEN-HAIM
Haifa, Israel

LESLIE BLACKFORD
Munfordville, Kentucky

KIM CAVENDER
St. Albans, West Virginia

SARAH CHINEN
Honolulu, Hawaii

IRIT COHEN
Binyamina, Israel

RHONDA COLCORD
Winter Springs, Florida

LYNNE DE NIO
New Castle, Colorado

ANN DILLON
Hancock, New Hampshire

KATHLEEN DUSTIN
Contoocook, New Hampshire

MARYLU ELLIOTT
North Highlands, California

NATALIA GARCIA DE LEANIZ
Torrelodones, Spain

LINDLY HAUNANI
Cabin John, Maryland

BRURYA HOCHMAN
Binyamina, Israel

MASAKO INABE
Tokyo, Japan

JEANETTE KANDRAY
Columbus, Ohio

KIM KORRINGA
Mountain View, California

Z. KRIPKE
San Diego, California

MIRA KRISPIL (PINKI)
Ashdod, Israel

DEDE LEUPOLD
Bend, Oregon

KAREN LEWIS (KLEW)
Tehachapi, California

EILEEN LORING

LAURIE MACISAAC
Canada

SANDRA MCCAW
Westborough, New Hampshire

DANIEL TORRES MANCERA
Torrelodones, Spain

SUSAN MUELLER
Breckenridge, Colorado

DAWN NAYLOR
Worcester, Massachusetts

SHARON OHLHORST
Wellsville, Utah

JANA ROBERTS BENZON
Salt Lake City, Utah

JEANETTE RICHMOND
Spring Creek, Nevada

LYNNE ANN SCHARZENBERG
Ansonia, Connecticut

SARAH SHRIVER
Santa Rosa, California

KAREN SEXTON
Centennial, Colorado

CAROL SIMMONS
Fort Collins, Colorado

SHANE SMITH
Florissant, Colorado

BARBARA SPERLING
Chatham, New Hampshire

CYNTHIA TINAPPLE
Worthington, Ohio

WENDY WALLIN MALINOW
Portland, Oregon

SUSAN WALTER
Torrance, California

MELANIE WEST
Freedom, Maine

NAAMA ZAMIR
Zichron Yaacov, Israel

INDEX